# Corn

by Ann L. Burckhardt

**Reading Consultant:**
Robin Johnston
National Corn Growers Association

# Bridgestone Books
an Imprint of Capstone Press

Bridgestone Books are published by Capstone Press
818 North Willow Street, Mankato, Minnesota 56001
Copyright © 1996 by Capstone Press
Printed in the United States of America

*Library of Congress Cataloging-in-Publication Data*
Burckhardt, Ann, 1933-
   Corn/ by Ann L. Burckhardt
   p. cm.--(Early-reader science. Foods)
   Includes bibliographical references (p. 24) and index.
   Summary: Simple text introduces corn, and instructions are given for making a corn husk wreath.
   ISBN 1-56065-450-3
   1. Corn--Juvenile literature. 2. Nature craft--Juvenile literature. [1. Corn.]
   I. Title. II. Series.
SB191.M2B84  1996
641.3'315--dc20

                                        96-26570
                                        CIP
                                        AC

Photo credits
Capstone Press, cover.
Chuck Place, 4
Visuals Unlimited, 6
International Stock, 8, 14, 16
FPG, 10, 12, 20
Unicorn, 18

# Table of Contents

Words in **boldface** type in the text are defined in the Words to Know section in the back of this book.

## What Is Corn?

Corn is one of the world's most important crops. Corn is also called maize. That is an Indian word meaning life-giver.

## Different Kinds of Corn

There are many different kinds of corn. Sweet corn and popcorn are grown for people to eat. Dent and flint corn are grown for animal feed. Indian corn is used for decoration.

## Parts of Corn

Corn grows on a **stalk**. It has four main parts. They are the cob, husk, silk, and **kernels**. Most kernels are yellow. Indian corn has red, blue, and purple kernels.

## Where Corn Grows

More than half of the world's corn is grown in the United States. Corn is grown mostly in the Corn Belt. The Corn Belt is in the middle part of the country. Iowa is the top corn producer.

## How Corn Grows

Corn needs hot summers, rich soil, and plenty of rain to grow. Kernels are planted and sprout in about 10 days. A stalk grows from the kernel. Leafy husks grow from the stalk. Cobs of corn grow under the husks.

## Harvest

When the silk turns brown on sweet corn, it is time to **harvest**. This is usually about three weeks after the silk appears. The kernels will be filled with a milky liquid.

## How We Use Corn

Corn is cooked and eaten. It is also used to make many things. There are corn flakes, corn chips, corn oil, corn syrup, and popcorn.

## History

Corn is **sacred** to many Amercian Indians. They taught the Pilgrims how to plant corn. The corn harvest is the reason we celebrate Thanksgiving.

## Corn and People

Many Native Americans still celebrate the first corn harvest of the season at the green corn festival. There is also a building covered with corn cobs in Mitchell, South Dakota. It is called the Corn Palace.

**Hands On**: Make a Corn Husk Wreath

The husk is the outer covering of the corn cob. The husk is like a leaf. It is often used for decoration.

**You will need**
- a wire hanger
- dried corn husks

1. Bend the wire hanger into a circle. Leave the hook so you can hang up your wreath.
2. Bend one piece of husk in the shape of an upside-down U.
3. Take the two ends, wrap them around the hanger, and pull them through the loop they make.
4. Keep tying the husks until the hanger is full.
5. Shred the ends of the husks into smaller pieces.
6. You can glue ribbons, buttons, or small toys to your wreath.
7. Hang your finished wreath on a wall.

## Words to Know

**harvest**—gather a crop

**kernel**—the edible part of the corn

**sacred**—holy and important to religion

**stalk**—main supporting stem of a plant

# Read More

**Aliki**. *Corn is Maize*. New York: Thomas Crowell, 1976.

**Bial, Raymond**. *Corn Belt Harvest*. Boston: Houghton Mifflin, 1991.

**Selsam, Millicent**. *Popcorn*. New York: William Morrow, 1976.

**Watts, Franklin**. *Corn*. Chicago: Children's Press, 1977.

# Index

# ART
## HARCOURT
### EVERYWHERE

AUTHORS

**Jacqueline Chanda**

**Kristen Pederson Marstaller**

CONSULTANTS

**Katherina Danko-McGhee**

**María Teresa García-Pedroche**

**Harcourt**
SCHOOL PUBLISHERS

Orlando   Austin   New York   San Diego   Toronto   London

Visit *The Learning Site!*
**www.harcourtschool.com**

# Dear Young Artist,

**W**hat does the word *artist* mean to you? You may think of an artist as only a person who draws or paints. However, photographers, weavers, and sculptors are also artists. Do you think of yourself as an artist?

In this book, you will see art from all over the world and from many different time periods. As you learn about these artworks and the artists who created them, you will design and create your own artworks. You will paint a landscape, draw a portrait, and even carve a sculpture. Along the way, you may discover a new artist—you!

Sincerely,

*The Authors*

# CONTENTS

## Unit 1 Nature Inspires Art .................. 24
### Line, Shape, and Color

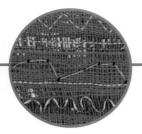

# Unit 4   Art Reflects Culture ............114

Pattern and Balance

# Unit 5    The Artist's Environment ...144
Space, Movement, and Unity

# AT A GLANCE

## Art Production

## Elements and Principles

## Cross-Curricular Connections

## Media

# Keeping a
# Sketchbook

**W**hen you make sketches and keep them together, you are keeping an art sketchbook. You can carry your sketchbook with you. Use it to make notes about your ideas, to sketch things you see, or to sketch what you imagine.

The artist Amedeo Modigliani created artworks of himself and the people around him in an unusual style.

◄ **Amedeo Modigliani,**
*Self-Portrait.*

In this sketch, Modigliani drew lines and shapes that may have been a plan for a sculpture. He used his sketches as a guide to create his sculptures.

**Amedeo Modigliani,** ▶
*Head of a Caryatid.*

Using a sketchbook is a good way to plan a finished artwork. You can sketch the composition of a painting, rearrange the parts of a sculpture, or experiment with patterns in a design. You can also practice your drawing skills.

You may want to collect poems, pictures, and textures that interest you. You can tape or glue them into your sketchbook. These things may give you ideas for art projects. If you write notes and dates next to your entries, your sketchbook will be a valuable resource for many years to come.

# Visiting a Museum

An art museum is a place where artworks are collected and displayed. You can find art museums in cities and towns all over the world.

**When you visit a museum, remember to**

- **Walk** slowly through the museum. Note the artworks that catch your eye.

- **Look** closely at the artworks, but don't touch them.

- **Think** about what each artist's message might be.

- **Listen** carefully to what the docent or guide tells you about the artworks.

- **Speak** quietly, but don't be afraid to ask questions.

▲ **The Parthenon**
**Nashville, Tennessee**

◀ **Guggenheim Museum**
**New York, New York**

*Fast Fact* Visitors to the Guggenheim Museum walk down a continuous spiraling ramp to view the artworks.

# Looking at Art

You may see artworks in museums, in books, or on websites. When you look at an artwork, you can follow these steps to better understand what you see:

- **DESCRIBE** Look closely at the artwork, and tell what you see. How would you describe the artwork to someone who has not seen it?

- **ANALYZE** Look at the way the artist organized the parts of the artwork. What part of it catches your eye first?

- **INTERPRET** Think about the idea or feeling the artist may be expressing in the artwork. Sometimes the title of an artwork can help you understand the artist's message.

- **EVALUATE** Use your observations about the artwork to form an opinion of it.

◀ **The Modern Art Museum of Fort Worth**

**Fort Worth, Texas**

*Fast Fact* The Modern Art Museum of Fort Worth, chartered in 1892, is the oldest art museum in Texas.

# Reading Your Textbook

**K**nowing how to read your art textbook will help you remember and enjoy what you read. Each lesson contains nonfiction text about artists, artworks, art techniques, and art history. Remember that nonfiction texts give facts about real people, things, events, or places.

The <u>title</u> tells the main topic of the lesson.

You can identify the most important ideas in each lesson by becoming familiar with the different features of your textbook. Look at this sample lesson from pages 48–51.

Highlighted words are art <u>vocabulary</u>.

## Lesson 5

**Vocabulary**

still life
overlapping
collage

**A** Paul Gauguin, *Still Life with Teapot and Fruit*, 1896, oil on canvas, 18¾ in. × 26 in. Metropolitan Museum of Art, New York, New York.

# Overlapping Shapes

### Still Life

Image **A** is an example of a **still life**. In a still life, objects, including flowers and food, are arranged in interesting ways. Which objects in image **A** appear to be the closest to the viewer? Which ones appear to be the farthest away?

The artist used **overlapping** to show that some objects are closer to the viewer than others. The objects in the back are partly covered by the objects in the front. The artist used overlapping to show that the teapot is in front of the flower. Where else did he use overlapping?

Captions next to each artwork give information such as the artist's name and the title of the artwork. Captions may also provide information about an artwork's date, materials, dimensions, and location. Subheads can provide clues about the ideas found in different sections of a lesson.

**Captions give important information about each artwork.**

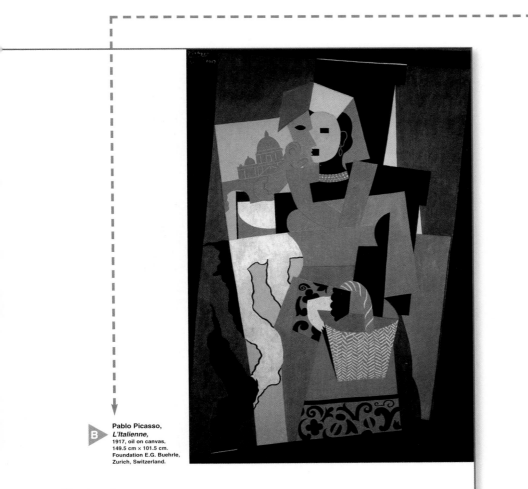

B  Pablo Picasso,
*L'Italienne*,
1917, oil on canvas,
149.5 cm × 101.5 cm.
Foundation E.G. Buehrle,
Zurich, Switzerland.

## Contract

Now look at image **B**. What is the subject of this artwork? Point out some details in the painting that tell about the subject. Look at the colors and shapes in image **B**. How did the artist use them to show contrast? Find examples of overlapping in the painting. Which object is the closest to the viewer? Which one is the farthest away?

**Subheads signal the beginning of a new section of text.**

49

# Reading Your Textbook

Other features of your textbook link artworks to related subject areas. Questions at the end of each lesson help you think about what you have learned.

**Links give facts related to an artist or an artwork.**

**Think Critically questions assess what you have learned.**

**This logo** 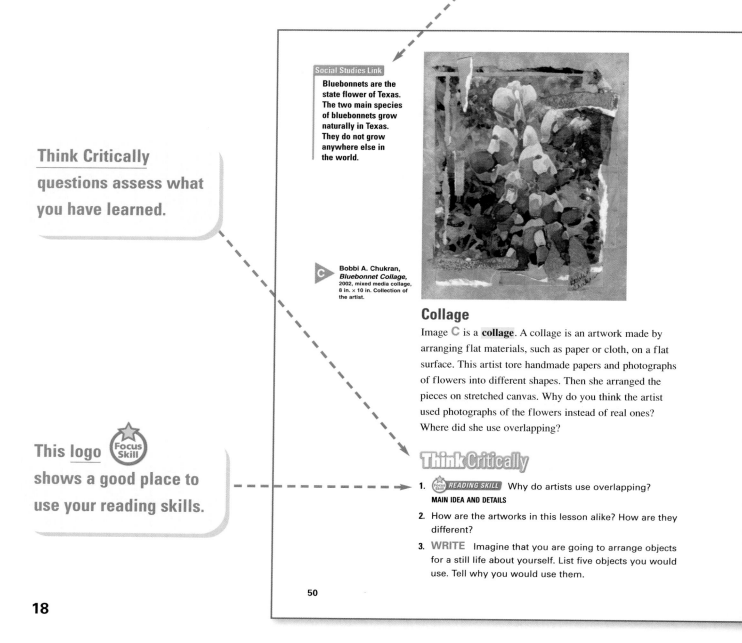 **shows a good place to use your reading skills.**

**Social Studies Link**

Bluebonnets are the state flower of Texas. The two main species of bluebonnets grow naturally in Texas. They do not grow anywhere else in the world.

C Bobbi A. Chukran, *Bluebonnet Collage,* 2002, mixed media collage, 8 in. × 10 in. Collection of the artist.

## Collage

Image **C** is a **collage**. A collage is an artwork made by arranging flat materials, such as paper or cloth, on a flat surface. This artist tore handmade papers and photographs of flowers into different shapes. Then she arranged the pieces on stretched canvas. Why do you think the artist used photographs of the flowers instead of real ones? Where did she use overlapping?

### Think Critically

1. (Focus Skill) **READING SKILL** Why do artists use overlapping? **MAIN IDEA AND DETAILS**

2. How are the artworks in this lesson alike? How are they different?

3. **WRITE** Imagine that you are going to arrange objects for a still life about yourself. List five objects you would use. Tell why you would use them.

**You can find more resources in the Student Handbook:**

- Maps of Museums and Art Sites, pp. 206–209
- Art Safety, pp. 210–211
- Art Techniques, pp. 212–227
- Elements and Principles, pp. 228–239
- Gallery of Artists, pp. 240–253
- Glossary, pp. 254–261
- Art History Time Line, pp. 262–263

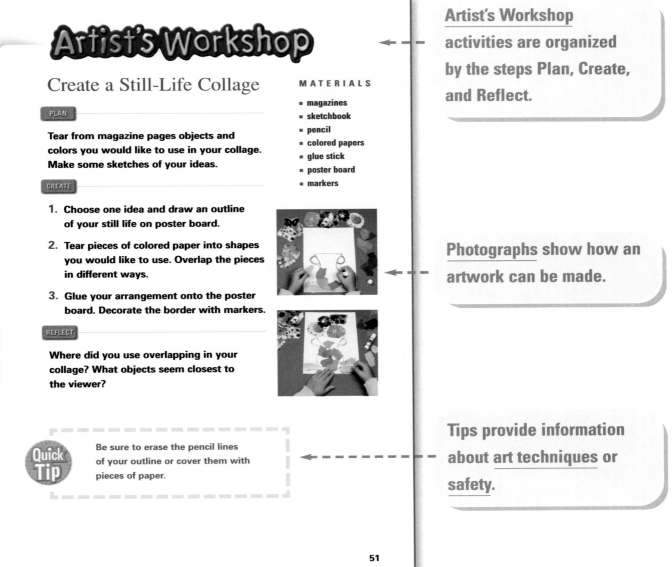

## Artist's Workshop

### Create a Still-Life Collage

**MATERIALS**
- magazines
- sketchbook
- pencil
- colored papers
- glue stick
- poster board
- markers

**PLAN**

Tear from magazine pages objects and colors you would like to use in your collage. Make some sketches of your ideas.

**CREATE**

1. Choose one idea and draw an outline of your still life on poster board.

2. Tear pieces of colored paper into shapes you would like to use. Overlap the pieces in different ways.

3. Glue your arrangement onto the poster board. Decorate the border with markers.

**REFLECT**

Where did you use overlapping in your collage? What objects seem closest to the viewer?

**Quick Tip**
Be sure to erase the pencil lines of your outline or cover them with pieces of paper.

Artist's Workshop activities are organized by the steps Plan, Create, and Reflect.

Photographs show how an artwork can be made.

Tips provide information about art techniques or safety.

51

# Elements and Principles

## Elements of Art

The **elements of art** are the basic parts of an artwork. You can use them to describe art and to plan and create your own artworks. As you look at these photographs, think about other places where you have seen the elements of art.

**SHAPE ▲**

an object that has height and width

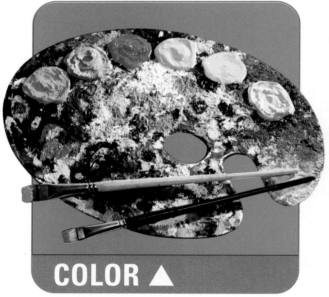

**COLOR ▲**

what we see when light is reflected off objects

**LINE ▲**

a mark that begins at one point and continues for a certain distance

See also Elements and
Principles, pages 228–239.

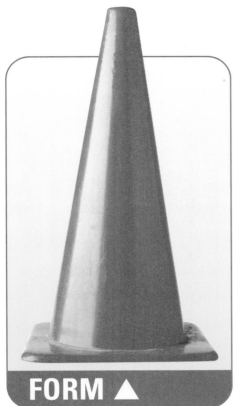

**FORM** ▲

an object that has height,
width, and depth

**TEXTURE** ▲

the way a surface looks or feels

**SPACE** ▲

the area around, between,
or within objects

**VALUE** ▲

the lightness or darkness of a color

21

# Principles of Design

Artists use the **principles of design** to arrange art elements in artworks. Look for the elements of art in these photographs. Think about how they are arranged and the effect this creates in each image.

**EMPHASIS** ▲

importance given to one part of an artwork

**VARIETY** ▲

the effect created by the use of different elements in an artwork to add interest

**MOVEMENT** ▲

the way the viewer's eyes travel from one element to another in an artwork

**UNITY** ▲

a sense that an artwork is complete and that its parts work together

See also Elements and Principles, pages 228–239.

## PROPORTION ▲

a sense that objects are the correct size in comparison to each other

## PATTERN ▲

a design made with repeated lines, shapes, or colors

## RHYTHM ▲

the visual beat created by the regular repeated elements in an artwork

## BALANCE ▲

the steady feeling created by the equal weight of elements on both sides

23

Robert S. Duncanson, *Loch Long,*
1867, oil on canvas, 17.7 cm × 30.3 cm.

**LOCATE IT**

This painting can be found at the Smithsonian American
Art Museum in Washington, D.C.

**See Maps of Museums and Art Sites, pages 206–209.**

Washington, D.C.

# Nature
## Inspires Art

## Step into the Art

Imagine that you could step into the scene in this painting. Where in the scene would you go first? What sounds would you hear? What would you see on the ground? Would you enjoy being in this scene? Why or why not?

**ABOUT THE ARTIST**

See Gallery of Artists, pages 240–253.

## Unit Vocabulary

| | | |
|---|---|---|
| landscapes | primary colors | cool colors |
| actual lines | secondary colors | seascape |
| implied lines | complementary colors | warm colors |
| geometric shapes | | still life |
| organic shapes | contrast | overlapping |
| close-up view | color scheme | collage |

**GO** ONLINE

**Multimedia Art Glossary**
Visit *The Learning Site*
www.harcourtschool.com

# Main Idea and Details

The *main idea* is what something is mostly about. *Details* give information to explain and support the main idea.

Look at the image below. The main idea of the painting is a summer morning on a farm. You can tell this is the main idea by looking at these details that support it.

- The title of the painting is *June Morning*.

- A farmer is milking his cow, and there is a barn in the background.

- The flowers are blooming.

**Thomas Hart Benton, *June Morning,***
1945, oil and tempera on masonite, $41\frac{7}{8}$ in. × $48\frac{1}{6}$ in.
**Cummer Museum of Art and Gardens, Jacksonville, Florida.**

Finding the main idea and details can also help you understand what you read. Read this passage. Think about what it is mostly about.

Thomas Hart Benton was an American artist who painted scenes of American life. He traveled around the country to see how people in rural areas lived. He got ideas from the people and scenes he saw. He sketched these scenes for his paintings. His paintings became well known for the way he showed rural American life.

What are the main idea and details in the passage? You can use a diagram like this to help you organize your thoughts.

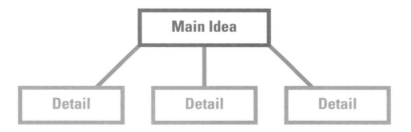

## On Your Own

As you read the lessons in this unit, use diagrams like the one above to find the main idea and details in the text and in the artworks. Look back at your completed diagrams when you see questions with **Focus Skill** *READING SKILL*.

# Lines in Landscapes

Artists often get ideas for artwork from nature. They may paint **landscapes**, or paintings of outdoor scenes.

## Kinds of Lines

Artists use many kinds of lines to create landscapes. Look at image **A**. The artist painted this outdoor scene in a way that does not look realistic, or like the actual scene. She used many different kinds of lines. What kinds of lines do you see? Where do you see thin, thick, long, short, or wavy lines? Point out some horizontal lines—straight lines that go from side to side. Read the title of image **A**. How did the artist use lines to show a windy day?

**A** **Maureen Golding,** *Windy Day in England,* 1991, gouache on paper, 12½ in. × 16 in. Private collection.

## Actual and Implied Lines

In image **B** the artist used thick, bold lines to outline the objects in his painting. Lines that outline objects are called **actual lines**.

Now compare image **C** to image **B**. What is the subject of both paintings? Do you see actual lines in image **C**? The edges of the objects in image **C** are suggested by **implied lines**.

If the artist had used actual lines to outline the objects in image **C**, would the painting look more realistic or less realistic?

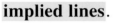 

B Alexej von Jawlensky, *Landscape of Murnau,* 1912, oil on canvas, 48.05 cm × 53.5 cm. Private collection.

 José María Velasco, *A Small Volcano in Mexican Countryside,* 1887, oil on canvas. Narodni Galerie, Prague, Czech Republic.

**LOCATE IT**

*Spiral Jetty* can be found in the Great Salt Lake in Utah.

Great Salt Lake

**UTAH**

**See Maps of Museums and Art Sites, pages 206–209.**

# Environmental Artwork

Have you ever seen anything in nature like the object in image ? The artist used nature itself to create this environmental artwork. Environmental art is made from materials found in nature and placed in a natural setting. What materials did the artist use? How did he show actual lines?

**D** **Robert Smithson,** *Spiral Jetty,*
1970, black rock, salt crystals, earth, red water (algae),
3 ft. × 15 ft. × 1500 ft. Great Salt Lake, Utah.

## Think Critically

1. **READING SKILL** What kinds of lines can artists use in landscapes? **MAIN IDEA AND DETAILS**

2. If you were drawing a realistic landscape, would you use more implied lines or more actual lines?

3. **WRITE** Think of a place where you would like to create an environmental artwork. Describe the artwork you would create.

# Artist's Workshop

## Draw a Landscape

**PLAN**

Find a picture of an outdoor place. Make some sketches for a landscape. Brainstorm the kinds of lines you will use. Plan the details in your painting.

**CREATE**

1. Select the sketch you like best. Copy it onto white paper.

2. Use colored pencils or markers to complete your landscape.

3. Include a variety of lines in your drawing.

**REFLECT**

What kinds of lines did you use in your landscape? Did you use more implied lines or more actual lines?

**Quick Tip**

As you brainstorm kinds of lines, draw them on a scrap of paper. Choose from these lines to draw your landscape.

# Shapes in Nature

Some artists paint full landscapes of natural scenes. Other artists focus on certain natural objects as subjects for their artworks. Look at images **A** and **B**. What do you see in each painting?

## Shapes

Each artist used different shapes to show his subject. Find the triangles in image **A**. Artists use lines with regular borders to paint **geometric shapes** such as triangles and circles. **Organic shapes** are made up of curved, irregular lines. Look at image **B**. Do you see more organic shapes or more geometric shapes in this painting?

 **Franz Marc, *Monkey Frieze,***
1911, oil on canvas, 76 cm × 134.5 cm.
Hamburger Kunsthalle, Hamburg, Germany.

**Vincent van Gogh,** *Irises,*
1889, oil on canvas, 71.1 cm × 93 cm.
J. Paul Getty Museum, Los Angeles,
California.

# Natural Scenes

Look at the leaves in image **B**. Notice how the artist painted
most of the leaves bending in the same direction. Did the
artist use actual lines or implied lines to paint them? Follow
the direction of the lines. Where do the lines lead your eyes?

The artist used diagonal, or slanted, lines to create the
sense that the leaves and flowers are moving. What would
image **B** look like if all the lines were vertical, or straight
up and down? Point out the diagonal lines in image **A**. In
which direction do they lead your eyes?

## Close-Up View

Look at images **C** and **D**. What is the subject of these images? Look back at the subject in image **B**. Compare it to image **C**. In image **B** the artist showed a large group of flowers. He painted them from far away. In image **C** the artist showed a **close-up view** of only two flowers. Painting a close-up view of a subject allows the viewer to see its details. Describe the shapes you see in images **C** and **D**.

 Georgia O'Keeffe, *Poppies,*
1950, oil on canvas, 36 in. × 30 in.
Milwaukee Art Museum, Milwaukee,
Wisconsin.

 Kirstie, grade 4,
*Prairie Flower.*

## Think Critically

1. **READING SKILL** What kinds of shapes are most often found in nature? **MAIN IDEA AND DETAILS**

2. What is the difference between geometric shapes and organic shapes?

3. **WRITE** Think about a nature scene you would like to paint. Tell how you would use shapes to show objects in your scene.

# Artist's Workshop

## Paint a Close-Up View

**PLAN**

Choose an object with an interesting close-up view. Make some sketches of the object from different angles. Look closely at the shapes that make up the object. Decide whether they are organic shapes or geometric shapes.

**CREATE**

1. Choose the sketch that shows the close-up view best.

2. Draw the object as large as possible on white paper. Try to fill the page.

3. Lightly outline each shape in pencil.

4. Choose your colors and paint the shapes.

**REFLECT**

Point out the different kinds of shapes you used.

### MATERIALS

- natural objects, such as plants or fruit
- sketchbook
- pencil
- white paper
- tempera paint
- paintbrushes
- water bowl

**Quick Tip**

Make the shapes in your close-up view stand out by outlining them in black marker.

# PICTURES OF THE PAST

**How do both nature and artists show us pictures of the past?**

A Mazon Creek fossil: shrimp-like animal.

B Mazon Creek fossil: plant frond.

Fossils are like pictures of the past. They show us how living things once looked. Many fossils can be found in rock. When a plant or an animal dies, the soft parts soon decay, or rot away. However, the harder parts may become buried over time. Parts that are saved like this are fossils.

Look at the fossil in image A. Does it look like any kind of animal you have seen before? This animal from the past was like a shrimp. What else do you notice about this fossil? Now look at the fossil in image B. Point out the stem and leaves.

Just as nature shows us images of the past, artists also show us images. Their images are from their own lives or the world around them. They capture a moment in time, whether real or imagined, and they save it for the future.

36

Georgia O'Keeffe, *Summer Days*,
1936, Oil on canvas, 36 in. x 30 in.
Whitney Museum of American Art,
New York, New York.

Georgia O'Keeffe was a twentieth-century artist who captured the beauty of nature in her paintings. In image C, O'Keeffe contrasts the bones of an animal with flowers and the desert sky. Why do you think she found beauty in these objects? How do images A, B, and C show us pictures of the past?

Suppose you were painting a picture for someone in the future. What would you want him or her to know about you or your world?

### DID YOU KNOW?

Scientists who study fossils are called paleontologists. They learn from fossils what plants or animals were like, what they ate, and how they died. This information is important to understand what happened on Earth in the past.

# Color Schemes

**primary colors**

**secondary colors**

**complementary colors**

**contrast**

**color scheme**

## Primary Colors

Red, blue, and yellow are **primary colors**. They are the most basic colors, because you cannot mix any other colors to get them. The primary colors are the building blocks for every color we see.

Find the primary colors on the color wheel on page 39. Then point out the primary colors in image .

**A** Paul Sierra,
***Elegy for Summer,***
1995, oil on canvas,
80 in. × 60 in. Collection
of Mr. Rudy Elias.

Robert Wagstaff,
*Visitors to the Rainforest,*
2001, gouache on board,
12 in. × 18 in. Collection
of the artist.

## Secondary Colors

**Secondary colors** are created by mixing two primary colors together. For example, yellow and blue mixed together make green. Orange, green, and violet are secondary colors. What two primary colors mixed together make orange? What color do you get when you mix red and blue?

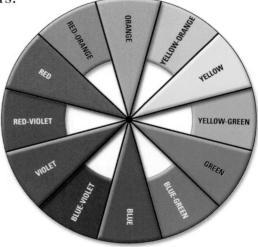

**Color Wheel**

## Complementary Colors

Colors such as red and green are opposite each other on the color wheel. They are called **complementary colors**. Complementary colors can be used together to create **contrast**, or a sharp difference between colors. Artists use contrast to guide a viewer's eyes toward certain parts of an artwork. Look at image . What do you notice first? Which colors are complementary?

Social Studies Link

Colleen Meechan's paintings often focus on her home state, Hawaii.

HAWAII

PACIFIC OCEAN

# Color Schemes

A **color scheme** is an artist's plan for choosing colors for an artwork. An artist might use a complementary color scheme to show contrast. Look at image **C**. Does the palm tree look realistic? Why or why not? In image **C**, the artist used colors that are not normally seen in nature. What do you think of the colors she chose?

 Colleen Meechan, *Blue Fronds,* 2001, acrylic on canvas, 42 in. × 48 in. Collection of the artist.

## Think Critically

1. **Focus Skill** *READING SKILL*  Why are primary colors important? **MAIN IDEA AND DETAILS**

2. Why might an artist paint an object in colors not usually seen in nature?

3. **WRITE**  Think of a place you know well. Then write a paragraph telling how you would paint it in unusual colors.

# Artist's Workshop

## Paint with Complementary Colors

### MATERIALS

- sketchbook
- pencil
- white paper
- tempera paint
- paintbrushes
- water bowl

**PLAN**

Think of an outdoor scene you would like to paint using complementary colors. Make a sketch of the scene. Then choose pairs of complementary colors to use in your painting.

**CREATE**

1. Using your sketch as a guide, draw the scene on white paper.

2. Paint your scene. Use complementary colors next to each other to show contrast.

**REFLECT**

Point out how you used complementary colors. Explain how you decided where to use contrast in your scene.

To keep your colors bright, remember to rinse your brush very well before using a new color.

# Color and Mood

**Vocabulary**

cool colors

seascape

warm colors

## Cool Colors

Artists may choose certain colors to create a mood, or feeling, in their artworks. Look at image **A**. What kind of mood did the artist create in this painting? What colors did the artist use? Blue, green, and violet are **cool colors**. They create a calm, peaceful mood.

Image **A** is a **seascape**. A seascape shows the sea, the sky, and sometimes the land. Why do you think seascapes are usually painted with cool colors?

**A** Claude Monet, *The Beach at Sainte-Adresse,* 1867, oil on canvas, 75.8 cm × 102.5 cm. The Art Institute of Chicago, Chicago, Illinois.

## Warm Colors

Look at image **B**. What kind of mood did the artist create
in this painting? Image **B** was painted with mostly
**warm colors**. Warm colors create a mood of warmth and
energy. Red, yellow, and orange are warm colors. Compare
the mood in image **B** with the mood in image **A**. What is
the setting of image **B**? Why do you think the artist chose
warm colors for this painting?

**Ole Juul Hansen, *Possibilities*,**
2002, crayon and watercolor on paper,
20 cm × 12.5 cm. Collection of the artist.

## Color and Contrast

Look closely at image **C**. Describe the scene. What colors did the artist use? Sometimes artists use both warm and cool colors to contrast different moods. What two moods did the artist contrast in image **C**?

## Think Critically

1. **READING SKILL**  How would you use color to express a peaceful mood? **MAIN IDEA AND DETAILS**

2. When might an artist use warm colors to paint a seascape?

3. **WRITE**  Imagine you are the man in image **C**. Write a paragraph describing the changes you feel as you move across the scene.

# Artist's Workshop

## Paint a Seascape or a Desert Landscape

**MATERIALS**

- magazines
- sketchbook
- pencil
- white paper
- tempera paint
- paintbrushes
- water bowl

**PLAN**

Look through magazines for pictures of seascapes and desert landscapes. Choose either one to draw. Then write a list of words to describe that kind of place. Sketch a couple of ideas based on your list of words.

**CREATE**

1. Select the sketch you like best, and copy it onto white paper.

2. Decide what mood you want to create. Choose warm colors or cool colors.

3. Paint your seascape or desert landscape.

**REFLECT**

How did you use color to create a feeling or mood? How did your list of words help you plan your painting?

After your painting is dry, you may want to add details with pastels.

**45**

# Paul Klee

## Why might two artists paint a landscape in different ways?

Paul Klee (KLAY) was born in Switzerland in 1879. As a boy, Klee drew landscapes and comic sketches. His parents felt he had artistic talent and sent him to art school.

Before Klee was born, most artists painted in a realistic style. They made the people and objects in their paintings look real. Klee wanted to do something different. He developed a style that showed his feelings. He used bold lines, simple shapes, and bright colors.

**A**    Paul Klee, *Moving Landscape,* 1920, oil on canvas, 31.5 cm x 49.5 cm. Private collection.

**Paul Klee,** *The Goldfish,* 1925, oil and watercolor on paper and board, 49.6 cm x 69.2 cm. Hamburger Kunsthalle, Hamburg, Germany.

Look at Klee's landscape painting in image **A**. Compare it to the landscape painting on pages 24–25. How are they different? What kinds of lines and shapes did Klee use in image **A**? Now look at image **B**. How would you describe the colors Klee used?

# Think About Art

Many of Klee's subjects came from nature. How do you see this idea in images **A** and **B**?

**Multimedia Biographies**
Visit *The Learning Site*
www.harcourtschool.com

## DID YOU KNOW?

**P**aul Klee was part of a group that called itself the Blue Rider. The group included painters, writers, poets, and composers of music. Blue Rider painters were known for their use of bright, exciting colors. The influence of the Blue Rider group can be seen in the work of some later artists.

# Overlapping Shapes

## Still Life

Image **A** is an example of a **still life**. In a still life, objects, including flowers and food, are arranged in interesting ways. Which objects in image **A** appear to be the closest to the viewer? Which ones appear to be the farthest away?

The artist used **overlapping** to show that some objects are closer to the viewer than others. The objects in the back are partly covered by the objects in the front. The artist used overlapping to show that the teapot is in front of the flower. Where else did he use overlapping?

**A** Paul Gauguin, *Still Life with Teapot and Fruit,* 1896, oil on canvas, $18\frac{3}{4}$ in. × 26 in. Metropolitan Museum of Art, New York, New York.

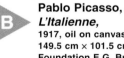 Pablo Picasso,
*L'Italienne,*
1917, oil on canvas,
149.5 cm × 101.5 cm.
Foundation E.G. Buehrle,
Zurich, Switzerland.

## Contrast

Now look at image **B**. What is the subject of this artwork?
Point out some details in the painting that tell about the
subject. Look at the colors and shapes in image **B**. How
did the artist use them to show contrast? Find examples of
overlapping in the painting. Which object is the closest to
the viewer? Which one is the farthest away?

49

Bluebonnets are the state flower of Texas. The two main species of bluebonnets grow naturally in Texas. They do not grow anywhere else in the world.

Bobbi A. Chukran, *Bluebonnet Collage,* 2002, mixed media collage, 8 in. × 10 in. Collection of the artist.

## Collage

Image **C** is a **collage**. A collage is an artwork made by arranging flat materials, such as paper or cloth, on a flat surface. This artist tore handmade papers and photographs of flowers into different shapes. Then she arranged the pieces on stretched canvas. Why do you think the artist used photographs of the flowers instead of real ones? Where did she use overlapping?

## Think Critically

1. **READING SKILL** Why do artists use overlapping?
   **MAIN IDEA AND DETAILS**

2. How are the artworks in this lesson alike? How are they different?

3. **WRITE** Imagine that you are going to arrange objects for a still life about yourself. List five objects you would use. Tell why you would use them.

# Artist's Workshop

## Create a Still-Life Collage

**MATERIALS**

- magazines
- sketchbook
- pencil
- colored papers
- glue stick
- poster board
- markers

**PLAN**

Tear from magazine pages objects and colors you would like to use in your collage. Make some sketches of your ideas.

**CREATE**

1. Choose one idea and draw an outline of your still life on poster board.

2. Tear pieces of colored paper into shapes you would like to use. Overlap the pieces in different ways.

3. Glue your arrangement onto the poster board. Decorate the border with markers.

**REFLECT**

Where did you use overlapping in your collage? What objects seem closest to the viewer?

**Quick Tip**

Be sure to erase the pencil lines of your outline or cover them with pieces of paper.

51

# Unit 1 Review and Reflect

## Vocabulary and Concepts

**Choose the letter of the word or phrase that best completes each sentence.**

**1** Triangles, rectangles, and squares are examples of ___.

**A** actual lines    **C** contrast

**B** organic shapes    **D** geometric shapes

**2** An artwork that shows an outdoor scene is called a ___.

**F** still life    **H** collage

**G** landscape    **J** contrast

**3** A ___ is an artist's plan for choosing colors.

**A** primary color    **C** still life

**B** color scheme    **D** contrast

**4** Artists use ___ to show one object in front of another.

**F** overlapping    **H** geometric shapes

**G** organic shapes    **J** contrast

**5** ___ colors can create a calm, peaceful mood in an artwork.

**A** Complementary    **C** Warm

**B** Primary    **D** Cool

## Focus Skill READING SKILL

## Main Idea and Details

**Reread the information about fossils in the first paragraph on page 36. Use a diagram like this to find the main idea and details.**

Main Idea

Detail    Detail    Detail

## Write About Art

Choose a piece of your own artwork, and write a paragraph about it. First, write about the main idea of your artwork. Then, write about the details that support the main idea. Use a diagram like the one on page 52 to plan your writing. Try to use unit vocabulary words in your paragraph.

**REMEMBER — YOU SHOULD**

- include only those details that support the main idea.

- use correct grammar, spelling, and punctuation.

## Critic's Corner

Look at *Man on a Bench* by Horace Pippin to answer the questions below.

Horace Pippin,
***Man on a Bench,***
1946, oil on fabric,
13 in. × 18 in.
Private collection.

**DESCRIBE** What is the subject of the artwork? How would you describe the subject?

**ANALYZE** Where do you see primary and complementary colors in the artwork? What kinds of lines do you see?

**INTERPRET** What kind of mood do you think the artist was trying to express?

**EVALUATE** Do you think the artist used colors and lines successfully to express the mood in this painting? Explain your answer.

Georges Seurat, *Bathers at Asnières*,
1883–1884, oil on canvas, 79 in. × 118$\frac{1}{2}$ in.

## LOCATE IT

This painting can be found at the National Gallery,
London, in the United Kingdom.

**See Maps of Museums and Art Sites, pages 206–209.**

UNITED
KINGDOM

London

# Moments in Time

## Step into the Art

Imagine you could step into the scene in this painting. What would the weather be like? What would the air smell like? What sounds would you hear? How would the water feel? Would you go for a swim?

## Unit Vocabulary

| | | |
|---|---|---|
| dominant color | tactile texture | gray scale |
| value | visual texture | blending |
| tints | fiber | emphasis |
| shades | Impressionism | three-dimensional |
| monochromatic | *plein air* | assemblage |
| | impasto | |

**GO ONLINE**

Multimedia Art Glossary
Visit *The Learning Site*
www.harcourtschool.com

## ABOUT THE ARTIST

See Gallery of Artists, pages 240–253.

# Fact and Opinion

A *fact* is a statement that can be proved. An *opinion* is a statement that expresses someone's thoughts or feelings.

Artists can show facts and opinions in their artworks. Look at the image below. The artist showed these facts in his painting:

• The weather is cold.

• Two cowhands and two horses are near a fence.

• There are no other people or animals in the scene.

Read the title of the painting. The artist may be expressing the opinion that it is sad that the cowhands' way of life is changing.

**Frederic S. Remington,** *The Fall of the Cowboy,*
1895, oil on canvas, 25 in. × 35$\frac{1}{8}$ in. Amon Carter Museum, Fort Worth, Texas.

Knowing the difference between facts and opinions can help you understand what you read. Read the passage below. Think about which statements are facts and which are opinions.

Frederic S. Remington was born on October 4, 1861, in Canton, New York. He went to school and then moved west and became a cowhand. He spent much of his life traveling through the western part of America, and he often drew or painted what he saw. It is important to study Remington's work to truly understand life in the American West. Remington's paintings and sculptures of the American West are the most interesting and beautiful in the world.

List the facts and opinions from the passage. You can use a chart like this one.

| Facts | Opinions |
|-------|----------|
|       |          |

# On Your Own

As you read the lessons in this unit, use charts to keep track of facts and opinions in the text and in the artworks. Look back at your charts when you see questions with Focus Skill *READING SKILL*.

# Color and Value

Vocabulary

dominant color

value

tints

shades

monochromatic

## Dominant Color

Look at the still-life painting in image . What objects do you see? What color do you notice first? The color you see most in an artwork is the **dominant color**. The artist of image **A** used mostly the color red to create a dominant color scheme.

**A** Meredith Brooks Abbott, *Kathy's Bowl,* 1993, oil on linen, 11 in. × 14 in. Private collection.

**B** Henri Rousseau,
*The Banks of the Bièvre
near Bicêtre,*
1904, oil on canvas, 21 in. × 18 in.
The Metropolitan Museum of Art,
New York, New York.

## Color and Mood

Now look at image **B**. What is the
dominant color in this painting? Is
it a warm color or a cool color?
What kind of mood, or feeling,
do you think the artist was trying
to express in this painting?
Compare image **A** to image **B**.
Do you get a different feeling
from image **A** than you do from
image **B**? Why do you think this
is so?

shades                                    tints

## Value

**Value** is the lightness or darkness of a color. Artists can
make lighter values, or **tints**, by mixing white with a color.
They can make darker values, or **shades**, by mixing black
with a color. The diagram above shows some tints and
shades of green. Find these tints and shades in image **B**.
Look at the way the artist used value to show shadows.
Where do you see tints and shades of red in image **A**?

**LOCATE IT**

The painting in image
**B** is located in the
Metropolitan Museum
of Art in New York,
New York.

**NEW YORK**

**New York City**

See Maps of Museums
and Art Sites,
pages 206–209.

59

# Monochromatic Color Scheme

Image C shows an example of a monochromatic color scheme. Look at the word *monochromatic*. *Mono* means "one," and *chrome* means "color." A **monochromatic** color scheme shows a group of values of one color. In image C, where did the artist use different values of the color he chose? What kind of mood do you get from image C?

Josef Albers,
***Homage to the
Square/Red Series,
Untitled III,***
1968, oil on masonite,
32 in. × 32 in. Norman
Simon Museum, Pasadena,
California.

## Think Critically

1. **(Focus Skill) *READING SKILL*** State one fact about image C. What is your opinion of this painting? **FACT AND OPINION**

2. What is the difference between a dominant color scheme and a monochromatic color scheme?

3. **WRITE** Write a paragraph telling what it would be like to walk through the scene in image B. Describe the mood of the scene.

# Artist's Workshop

## Create a Monochromatic Painting

**MATERIALS**

- pencil
- sketchbook
- white paper
- tempera paint
- paintbrushes
- water bowl
- paper plates

### PLAN

Think of an object you would like to paint. Make some sketches of your object. Choose one color to use.

### CREATE

1. Copy your best sketch onto white paper.

2. On a paper plate, mix tints and shades of the color you chose. Decide where you want to use these values in your painting.

3. Paint your object. Use as many tints and shades as you can.

### REFLECT

Point out the tints and shades you used in your painting.

**Quick Tip**

You can include pure white and pure black in a monochromatic painting.

61

# Natural Textures

## Tactile Texture and Visual Texture

Have you ever touched the bark of a tree? How would you describe what you felt? The surface of a real object has **tactile texture**. This is what the object feels like when you touch it. Look at image **A**. The artist has used line, color, and value to create visual texture. **Visual texture** shows the appearance of texture on a drawn or painted surface. How would you describe the texture you see in image **A**?

 **Chris Kenny,**
***Flowering Tree,***
1992, oil on canvas,
152 cm × 122 cm.
Private collection.

# Value and Texture

The artist used value in image **A** to show a rough texture. Notice the way shades were used to show deep grooves in the bark of the tree.

Now describe the visual texture in image **B**. How is it different from the visual texture in image **A**? Notice how the artist used tints and shades to show a smooth, silky texture. What does the title of image **B** tell you about the cat's texture?

**B** Isy Ochoa, *Velvet Cat I*, 1996, oil on canvas, 30 cm × 30 cm. Private collection.

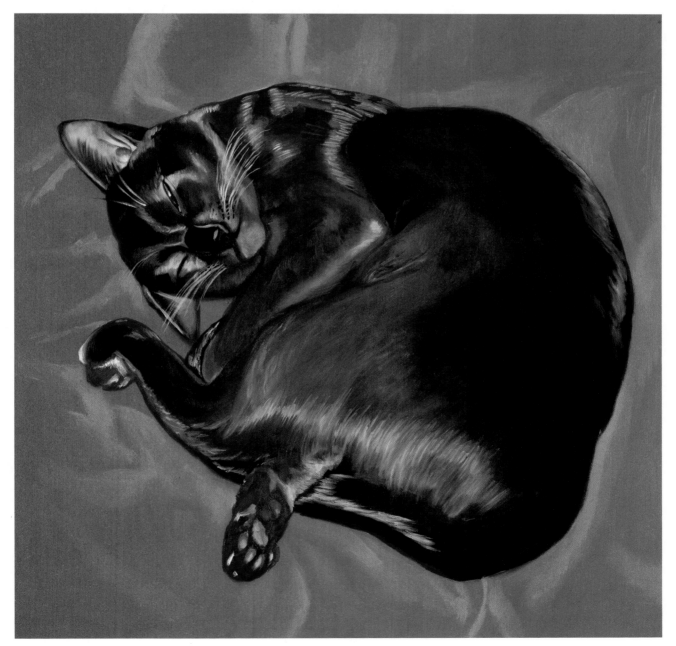

**Think about the smooth surface of a piece of notebook paper. A smooth surface reflects light evenly. Now think about crumpling that piece of notebook paper to give it a rough surface. A rough surface reflects the light unevenly, creating more dark values. The way light is reflected by a surface shows values and textures.**

# Fibers Create Texture

Describe the artwork in image **C**. This artwork was made with different kinds of fibers. A **fiber** is thread or a similar material, such as yarn or string. What do you think the tactile texture of the artwork in image **C** is like?

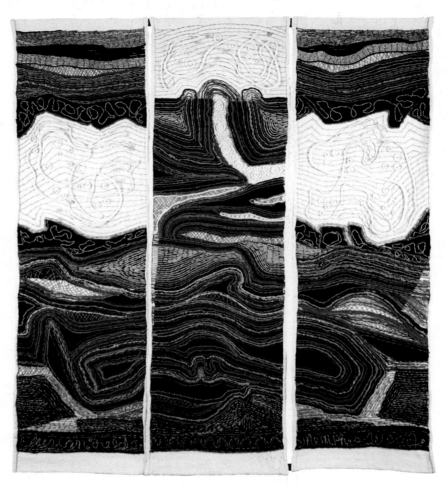

**C** **Memphis Wood,**
*Elysian Fields,*
1978, mixed fibers,
96 in. × 88 in. (each panel
96 in. × 27$\frac{1}{2}$ in.) Jacksonville
Museum of Modern Art,
Jacksonville, Florida.

## Think Critically

1. **READING SKILL** How do you think the artist of image **B** feels about cats? Explain your answer using details from the painting. **FACT AND OPINION**

2. Explain how artists use value to create visual texture.

3. **WRITE** Choose an object in your classroom to describe in a riddle. Write clues that describe the object's texture. Ask a classmate to read your riddle and to guess the object you chose.

# Artist's Workshop

## Create Texture in a Collage

**MATERIALS**

- objects with different textures
- tissue paper
- crayons
- scissors
- glue
- poster board
- yarn or string

**PLAN**

Find objects with different textures, such as a feather, a sponge, a group of toothpicks, or the sole of a shoe.

**CREATE**

1. Use different colors of crayons to do a rubbing of each object on tissue paper.

2. Cut out your rubbings and decide how you want to arrange them in a collage.

3. Glue the rubbings onto a piece of poster board.

**REFLECT**

What kinds of visual textures are in your collage?

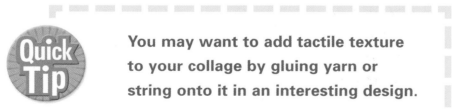

**Quick Tip**

You may want to add tactile texture to your collage by gluing yarn or string onto it in an interesting design.

# EROSION

*What kinds of textures do you see and feel around you? How might textures change over time?*

Think about the textures found in nature. The textures of some landforms and rocks have been made by a process called erosion. Erosion is the wearing away of rock and other materials by wind and moving water.

Image A shows one example of erosion. Wave Rock is about 50 feet high. How do you think it got its name? For millions of years, water carrying minerals such as iron ran down over the rock, cutting lines into it. The minerals also added streaks of color to the rock. What kind of texture do you think Wave Rock has? What colors can you see in it?

A Wave Rock, **Western Australia.**

Image **B** shows rock that has been worn away by ocean water and wind as well as by rainwater. How would you describe the texture of the landform in image **B**?

# THINK ABOUT ART

Find several objects in your school that have different textures. What words would you use to describe each texture?

## DID YOU KNOW?

**E**rosion affects buildings as well as landforms. Some buildings can stand up to erosion better than others because of their design. The pyramid shown below is about 4,600 years old. Wind moves up along its flat, angled sides instead of hitting them directly. This keeps the wind and the blowing sand from doing a lot of damage to the pyramids. The design of pyramids has reduced their erosion over the centuries.

**C** **Pyramid of Cheops (Khufu),** Giza, Egypt.

# Light and Color

## Impressionism

The same building is shown in both image **A** and image **B**. How are the two paintings alike? How are they different? Read the title of each painting. How did the artist use color to show two different times of day?

These artworks were painted in the late nineteenth century in a style called **Impressionism**. The Impressionists were not interested in painting exact details. They wanted to show the way light and color looked at a certain moment in time. How do you think the artist of images **A** and **B** would show the building at sunset?

 Claude Monet, *Rouen Cathedral, Impression of Morning,*
1894, oil on canvas, 0.91 m × 0.63 m.
Musée d'Orsay, Paris, France.

 Claude Monet, *Rouen Cathedral, Bright Sun,*
1894, oil on canvas, 0.91 m × 0.63 m.
Musée d'Orsay, Paris, France.

 **Berthe Morisot, *The Butterfly Hunt,***
1874, oil on canvas, 22 in. × 18 in.
Musée d'Orsay, Paris, France.

# Outdoor Painters

The Impressionists often painted outdoors. Outdoor painting is called ***plein air*** (PLAYN AIR), which is French for "open air." Artists had usually painted outdoor scenes indoors, from memory. The Impressionists painted from real life instead. They painted very quickly to capture an impression of their subjects. Look at the painting in image **C**, and read the title. Why do you think the artist had to paint this subject very quickly?

**LOCATE IT**

Images **A**, **B**, and **C** can be found in the Musée d'Orsay, a museum in Paris, France.

See Maps of Museums and Art Sites, pages 206–209.

## Everyday Themes

Look at image **D**. What do you see? The Impressionist
painter captured a moment in his subjects' lives.
Impressionism often focused on people doing ordinary
things they enjoyed. Notice the thick brushstrokes in this
painting. This technique, known as **impasto** (im•PAS•toh),
gave the painting a bumpy tactile texture. Where do you see
light and dark values? What time of day do you think he
showed?

## Think Critically

1. **READING SKILL** Do you think a painting of an outdoor
   scene would look more interesting if it were painted
   outdoors or from memory indoors? **FACT AND OPINION**

2. How did the artist of image **D** use value to create the
   appearance of waves?

3. **WRITE** Write a description of image **D**. Tell what you
   might see, hear, smell, and feel if you were standing next
   to the girl with the hat.

# Artist's Workshop

## Paint an Outdoor Scene

**MATERIALS**

- magazines
- pencil
- sketchbook
- white paper
- tempera paint or watercolors
- paintbrushes
- water bowl

### PLAN

Find a picture in a magazine of an outdoor place you like. Notice the time of day in the picture. Make some quick sketches of the place, but don't be concerned with drawing the details.

### CREATE

1. Using your sketches as a guide, paint your outdoor scene.

2. Use color in your painting to show the time of day. Use light values to show sunlight and dark values to show shadows.

### REFLECT

How did you use value and color in your painting?

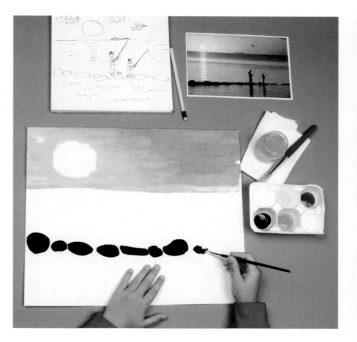

Try to use quick brushstrokes as the Impressionists did.

# Values of Black and White

Value is the lightness or darkness of a color. When only black, white, and gray are used in an artwork, the contrast between values is especially obvious.

## Gray Scale

Look at the gray scale below. A **gray scale** shows the gradual changes in value from pure black to pure white. In image **A**, point out the darkest and lightest values you can see. How would you describe the texture of image **A**?

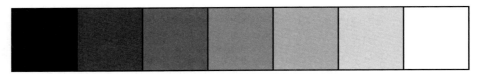

 Bruce Barnbaum,
*Dance of the Corn Lilies,*
1991, photograph.

72

**M. C. Escher, *Dewdrop,***
1946, mezzotint, 18 cm × 24.5 cm.
Cordon Art B. V., Baarn, Holland.

# Value and Texture

What is the subject of the artwork in image **B**? Notice the way the artist used value to show texture. Describe the visual texture of the leaf. Now look at the dewdrop. What do you think makes the dewdrop look wet?

## Value Changes

Look back at image **A**. Notice the sharp contrast in value from dark to light. Suppose an artist wanted to show gradual changes in value. The artist could use **blending**, or mixing, to create a smooth transition from dark to light. To blend the values in a charcoal drawing or in a painting, an artist can smudge darker areas to mix them with lighter areas. In image **C**, where do you find value changes?

## Think Critically

1. **Focus Skill** **READING SKILL**  Look at the title of image **A**. Is this a good title? Why or why not? **FACT AND OPINION**

2. What is a gray scale?

3. **WRITE**  Look at the objects in image **C**. If you wanted to create an artwork using these items, what type of artwork would you create? Describe your ideas.

Matthew, grade 4, Untitled.

# Artist's Workshop

## Draw a Charcoal Still Life

**PLAN**

Choose a group of objects to draw. Arrange the objects in an interesting way. Make some sketches of your still life. Decide how you want to use value in your charcoal drawing.

**CREATE**

1. Use a charcoal pencil to copy your best sketch onto white paper.

2. Use a range of dark and light values to show textures and shadows in your still life.

3. Create gradual value changes by using a tissue to smudge, or blend, areas of your artwork.

**REFLECT**

How did you use value in your drawing? Where did you use blending?

**MATERIALS**

- classroom objects
- pencil
- sketchbook
- white paper
- charcoal pencil
- tissue
- eraser

**Quick Tip**

You can use an eraser to remove some of the charcoal to create contrast between areas.

# Henri Matisse

*How does an artist explore the same idea in different kinds of art?*

Henri Matisse (ahn•REE mah•TEES) was born in France in 1869. He had no interest in art until he was twenty years old. Then his mother gave him a set of paints to keep him busy while he was sick. Soon after, Matisse began to work as an artist.

Look at image **B**. How would you describe the colors Matisse used in this painting? What kinds of textures did he show?

Matisse created many colorful paintings and sculptures, as well as illustrations for books. He also designed interiors of rooms and sets and costumes for ballets. In all of his art projects, color was the most important element. Matisse used color to express his positive feelings about his life and work.

**Henri Matisse,** *Self-Portrait,* 1918, oil on canvas, 65 cm x 54 cm. Private collection.

 **Henri Matisse,**
***Interior with Egyptian Curtain,***
1948, oil on canvas, 116.2 cm x 84.1 cm.
Phillips Collection, Washington, D.C.

Near the end of his life, Matisse
had health problems, but he did not
stop working. When painting became
too hard, he started small projects
that he could work on in bed, such as
collages. Look at image **C**. Matisse
created this collage by using paper
that he painted and then cut into
different shapes.

 **Henri Matisse,**
***The Trapeze Performers (Les Codomas),***
1947, gouache on paper cutouts, 42 cm x 65 cm.
National Museum of Modern Art, Georges
Pompidou Center, Paris, France.

# Think About Art

Look at the self-portrait of Matisse
in image **A**. What do you see in
this painting that might tell you
something about Matisse?

 **Multimedia Biographies**
Visit *The Learning Site*
www.harcourtschool.com

# Emphasis

Artists create emphasis in an artwork to grab the viewer's attention. **Emphasis** is the special importance given to a part of an artwork. It is created by using the elements of art to make one or more parts of an artwork stand out.

A  Raymond Depardon,
*Palm Tree in Mauritania,*
1999, photograph.

## Contrasting Values

Look at image A. How did the photographer create emphasis in this scene? The palm tree stands out because its dark value shows a contrast, or sharp difference, from the rest of the scene. Notice that the tree trunk is the only vertical line in the photograph. This also draws attention to the palm tree.

Now look at image B. What do you notice first? This artist used value to emphasize several areas in her artwork. Look at the light values in the moon, the wave, and the subject's hair. They stand out from the darker values in the sky, the water, and the subject's clothing.

B  Johanna Fiore,
*Portrait of Gordon Parks,*
1997, photograph.

 David Hockney, *A Bigger Splash,*
1967, acrylic on canvas, 96 in. × 96 in.
Tate Gallery, London, England.

# Contrasting Shapes

In image C, what catches your eye first? Most of this scene
is made up of geometric shapes. Notice the contrast created
by the organic shapes and lines in the splash of water.
Imagine this scene without the splash of water. What kind
of feeling would it create? How does the splash change the
mood of the painting?

**Cultural Link**

**The portrait in
image B is of Gordon
Parks, a photographer
who used his art to
show the everyday
lives of African
Americans. Parks won
many awards for his
accomplishments.**

# Emphasis in Three-Dimensional Art

Artists create emphasis in three-dimensional art just as they do in a two-dimensional painting or photograph. **Three-dimensional** artworks have height, width, and depth. Image **D** is a three-dimensional artwork called an assemblage. An **assemblage** is an artwork made from a variety of materials, such as paper and wood. How would you describe the textures in this artwork? Where do you see emphasis in image **D**?

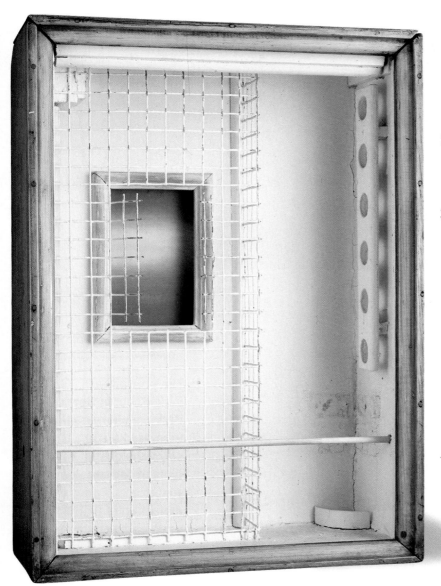

## Think Critically

1. **(Focus Skill) READING SKILL** State one fact and one opinion about the painting in image **C**.
   **FACT AND OPINION**

2. What kind of color scheme could you use to create emphasis in an artwork?

3. **WRITE** Tell why you think the artist of image **D** named his artwork *Toward the Blue Peninsula*.

**D** Joseph Cornell,
*Toward the Blue Peninsula,*
1951–1952, mixed media,
$10\frac{5}{8}$ in. × $14\frac{15}{16}$ in. × $3\frac{15}{16}$ in.
Collection of Daniel Varenne, Geneva, Switzerland.

# Create a Pastel Drawing

- magazines
- pencil
- sketchbook
- white paper
- oil pastels

**PLAN**

Choose a magazine photograph of a subject you like. Make sketches of your subject.

**CREATE**

1. Choose your best sketch, and draw it on white paper.

2. Decide how you want to use emphasis in your drawing. You could contrast values, shapes, colors, or textures.

3. Use oil pastels to complete your drawing.

**REFLECT**

What do you want viewers to notice first in your drawing? How did you create emphasis?

**Quick Tip**

You may add something surprising to your drawing, such as the splash in image C on page 79, to create emphasis.

# Unit 2 Review and Reflect

## Vocabulary and Concepts

**Choose the letter of the word or phrase that best completes each sentence.**

1 ___ is the lightness or darkness of a color.

   **A** Shade     **C** Impasto

   **B** Tint     **D** Value

2 ___ can be felt by touching.

   **F** Tactile texture     **H** Emphasis

   **G** Visual texture     **J** Value

3 A painting with ___ has a bumpy texture.

   **A** emphasis     **C** gray scale

   **B** dominant color     **D** impasto

4 A ___ shows values from black to white.

   **F** tactile texture     **H** blending

   **G** dominant color     **J** gray scale

5 Artists use ___ in an artwork to grab the viewer's attention.

   **A** texture     **C** value

   **B** emphasis     **D** impasto

## Focus Skill READING SKILL

### Fact and Opinion

**Write a paragraph about the painting on pages 54–55. Include at least one fact and one opinion. Exchange papers with a partner. Read your partner's paragraph. Then use a chart like this one to list the facts and opinions your partner wrote.**

| Facts | Opinions |
|-------|----------|
|       |          |

## Write About Art

Choose a piece of your artwork from this unit. Then write a paragraph that gives both facts and opinions about it. Use a chart like the one on page 82 to plan your writing.

**REMEMBER — YOU SHOULD**

- be able to prove the facts you write about.

- use correct spelling, punctuation, and grammar.

- try to use unit vocabulary words in your paragraph.

## Critic's Corner

Look at *Basket of Bread* by Salvador Dalí to answer the questions below.

**DESCRIBE** What facts about the artwork can you state?

**ANALYZE** How would you describe the different textures in this artwork?

**INTERPRET** How do the colors and textures affect the mood in this artwork?

**EVALUATE** What is your opinion of the artist's choice of subject in this artwork? What do you think of the way he showed his subject?

**Salvador Dalí, *Basket of Bread,***
1926, oil on wood panel, 12 in. × 12 in.
Dalí Museum, Reynolds Morse
Collection, St. Petersburg, Florida.

**Winslow Homer, *Children on a Fence,***
1874, watercolor over pencil on paper, 6 in. × 11 in.

## LOCATE IT

This painting can be found at the Williams College Museum of Art in Williamstown, Massachusetts.

**See Maps of Museums and Art Sites, pages 206–209.**

# People in Art

## Step into the Art

Imagine that you could step into this painting and join the children sitting on the fence. What do you think they would be talking about? What kinds of games do you think they might play? What would you like to ask them?

## Unit Vocabulary

| | | |
|---|---|---|
| portrait | Cubism | positive space |
| facial proportions | gesture drawing | negative space |
| self-portrait | rhythm | form |
| abstract art | relief sculpture | terra-cotta |
| distortion | subtractive method | |

**GO ONLINE**

Multimedia Art Glossary
Visit *The Learning Site*
www.harcourtschool.com

# Narrative Elements

*Narrative elements* are the parts of a story. They include the characters, setting, and plot. The *characters* are the people or animals in the story. The *setting* is when and where the story takes place. The *plot* is what happens in the story.

Artists may tell stories in their artworks. Look at the image below.

- The **characters** are the people working on the farm, as well as the animals.

- The **setting** is a farm in the country, perhaps long ago.

- The **plot** is what is happening on the farm.

Look at what the characters are doing and at details in the setting to help you understand the story the artist is telling.

Anna Pugh,
*A Day in the
Country,* 1993,
acrylic on board,
32 in. × 28 in.
Private collection.

Knowing the characters, setting, and plot can also help you understand the stories you read. Read this passage. Think about the narrative elements.

> "Now, Jack, be sure to get every one of those ripe apples before sundown," Dad said as he walked by with the wheelbarrow.
>
> "Do you think Mom will win the pie contest at the fair again this year, Dad?" asked Jack.
>
> "Of course she'll win! She's won every year for three years! But she'll need a lot of apples to make enough for the judges."
>
> "I just hope there's some left over for us this year," Jack said. "Last year the judges ate everything."
>
> Dad laughed. "Don't worry, Jack. It's a good crop this year. We'll be having pie after the fair for sure!"

What are the characters, setting, and plot? Use a story map like this one to help you.

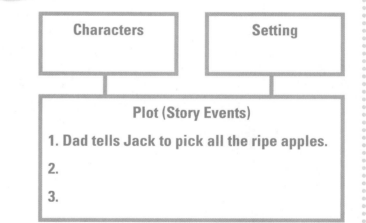

| Characters | Setting |
|---|---|

**Plot (Story Events)**

1. Dad tells Jack to pick all the ripe apples.

2.

3.

# On Your Own

As you look at the artworks in this unit, use story maps to record narrative elements in the artworks. Look back at your completed story maps when you see questions with **Focus Skill** *READING SKILL*.

# Proportion in Portraits

Images **A**, **B**, and **C** are portraits. A **portrait** is an artwork that shows a person, a group of people, or an animal. An artist creates a portrait to show how a subject looks or what a subject is like.

## Personality in Portraits

A portrait often reflects the subject's personality. An artist may experiment with lines, shapes, or colors to express the feelings and character of the subject. What do you think the artist wanted to show about the man in image **A**?

**A** **Alice Kent Stoddard,** *Young Man in Blue Suit,* about 1930, oil on canvas, 34 in. × 30 in. Collection of David David Gallery, Philadelphia, Pennsylvania.

**LOCATE IT**

The portrait in image **B** can be found in Florence, Italy.

**Florence**

**ITALY**

**See Maps of Museums and Art Sites, pages 206–209.**

**B** Agnolo Bronzino, *Portrait of Francesco I De'Medici,* 1551, tempera on wood panel, 58.5 cm × 41.5 cm. Uffizi Gallery, Florence, Italy.

## Facial Proportions

When an artist draws or paints a realistic portrait, he or she studies the subject's head, eyes, nose, and mouth. Then the artist shows the **facial proportions**, or how these features are related to each other in size and placement.

Notice the facial proportions in image **B**. Compare the boy's face with the diagram. The boy's eyes are about halfway between the top of his head and his chin. His nose is about halfway between his eyes and his chin, and his mouth is about halfway between his nose and his chin.

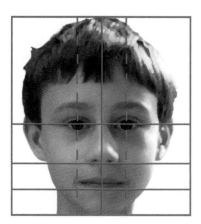

# Self-Portraits

**Self-portraits** are portraits that artists create of themselves. Image **C** is a self-portrait by Mexican artist Frida Kahlo. Each of Kahlo's many self-portraits expressed something about her personality. Kahlo added details to reflect her emotions. What can you tell about the artist by the details she included?

## Think Critically

1. **READING SKILL** Imagine that the boy in image **B** is a character in a story. What do you think he is like?
   **NARRATIVE ELEMENTS**

2. What is the difference between a portrait and a self-portrait?

3. **WRITE** Describe how you would show yourself in a self-portrait. What would you be wearing? What else would you put in the painting that would say something about you?

C Frida Kahlo,
***Self-Portrait with Loose Hair,***
1947, oil on masonite, 24 in. × 17¾ in.
Private collection.

# Artist's Workshop

## Draw a Portrait

- pencil
- sketchbook
- white paper
- colored pencils or markers

**PLAN**

Choose a classmate you would like to draw. Observe your classmate's facial features closely. Lightly sketch what you see. Look at the diagram of human facial proportions on page 89 to help you.

**CREATE**

1. Use your sketch as a guide to draw the portrait. Think about the size and placement of each facial feature.

2. Use colored pencils or markers to add color and details to your drawing.

3. Show something in your portrait about your classmate's personality.

**REFLECT**

How did you use facial proportions? Point out the details in your portrait that show something about your classmate.

Quick Tip

To check the proportions of facial features on your portrait, lightly draw the lines you see in the diagram on page 89. Erase these lines before you add color to your portrait.

# Abstract Portraits

Look at the portrait in image **A**. Trace the subject's nose with your finger. How does it compare with a real person's nose? Artists may use line, shape, and color in unusual ways to create images that look different from real life. This kind of art is called **abstract art**. How can you tell that image **A** is an abstract portrait?

Geometric shapes are commonly used in abstract art. What geometric shapes do you see in images **A**, **B**, **C**, and **D**?

The way an artist uses line, shape, and color in an abstract portrait might show the emotions of the subject in a way that realistic art cannot. What kind of feeling do you get from image **A**? What do you think the subject's mood was?

**A** Alexej von Jawlensky, *Mystical Head: Crow Wings (Mystischer Kopf: Rabenflügel),* 1918, oil on paper laid down on card, 10 in. × 7⅝ in.

Juan Gris, *Portrait of Picasso,*
1912, oil on canvas, 93.4 cm × 74.3 cm.
Art Institute of Chicago, Chicago, Illinois.

## Distortion and Cubism

Look again at image **A**. Think about the facial proportions.
Are the facial proportions in image **A** true to life? When
artists change the proportions from what a viewer might
expect, they are using **distortion**. Artists can distort the way
a subject looks by bending, stretching, or twisting parts of
the image. What parts of the face in image **A** are distorted?
How are they distorted?

Image **B** is an abstract portrait of the artist Pablo
Picasso, painted by the artist Juan Gris (GREES). Gris
admired Picasso's style of abstract painting, called **Cubism**.
Artists who painted in this style often showed more than
one view of a subject in the same image. Look closely at the
face of the subject in image **B**. Point out his eyes, nose, and
mouth. Can you see more than one view of the subject?

**LOCATE IT**

The portrait in
image **B** can be found
at the Art Institute of
Chicago in Chicago,
Illinois.

Chicago

ILLINOIS

See Maps of Museums
and Art Sites,
pages 206–209.

Look at image **C**. Do you recognize any of the objects in the painting? Read the painting's title. Look for objects such as the armchair and the woman's arms.

Now look at image **D**. What does it have in common with image **B**? How many different views of the subject's face do you see?

**C** Pablo Picasso, *Woman Seated in an Armchair,* 1917–1920, oil on canvas, $51\frac{3}{8}$ in. × 35 in.

## Think Critically

1. **READING SKILL** What is the subject of image **B** holding in his hand? What does it tell you about him? **NARRATIVE ELEMENTS**

2. How is image **D** like image **A**? How is it different?

3. **WRITE** Write a paragraph explaining your opinion about whether artists should study the works of other artists.

**D** Anna, grade four, Untitled.

94

# Artist's Workshop

## Create an Abstract Portrait

**MATERIALS**

- newspapers or magazines
- pencil
- sketchbook
- white paper
- oil pastels

**PLAN**

Choose a photograph of a person from a newspaper or magazine. Make some sketches of your subject's face.

**CREATE**

1. Select the sketch you like best.

2. Use your sketch to experiment with distortion by using geometric shapes for facial features. You may want to change the sizes of some of your subject's features.

3. Use oil pastels to draw the abstract portrait. Use lines and colors to show what your subject's personality might be like.

**REFLECT**

How did you use distortion? What does your portrait show about your subject's personality or emotions?

**Quick Tip**

Remember that cool colors in a portrait might show a quiet personality. Warm colors might show a lively personality.

95

# Portraits in Time

*How is posing for a portrait today different from posing for a portrait long ago?*

Diego Velázquez, *Las Meninas*, 1656, oil on canvas, 125 in. x $108\frac{3}{4}$ in. Museo del Prado, Madrid, Spain.

**B**efore photography was invented, portraits were usually painted. The subjects of most portraits were important people. They would sit for the portraits in elaborate clothing for many hours at a time.

Image A helps us imagine what it was like to pose for a portrait long ago. The artist has cleverly shown not only the subjects of the portrait but also their viewpoints. Both King Philip IV and Queen Mariana of Spain are reflected in the mirror on the back wall of the room. What do they see as they pose for their portrait? Where do you see a self-portrait of the artist, Diego Velázquez?

The young girl in the center of image A is Princess Margarita, the king and queen's daughter. Her maid seems to be encouraging her to pose for the painting. Why do you think the princess is unwilling to join her parents?

Image **B** is a photographic portrait of Sam Houston, the first and third president of the Republic of Texas. Having your portrait painted or photographed showed that you were important. Subjects often posed with objects that told something about them. Why do you think Sam Houston wanted to pose wearing a blanket and holding a walking stick?

# Think About Art

Think of a famous person you would like to paint. What objects would you include in your painting that might tell something about that person? Explain your answer.

The first successful kind of photograph, a daguerreotype (duh•GEH•roh•typ), was invented in the 1830s. Subjects of early photographs had to sit motionless for 3 to 15 minutes while chemicals in the camera were exposed to bright sunlight.

The daguerreotype below is of Frederick Douglass.

**Portrait of Frederick Douglass,** about 1850.

**Daguerreotype camera**

**B** **Photograph of Sam Houston,** about 1850s.

**GO ONLINE** **Multimedia Biographies** Visit *The Learning Site* www.harcourtschool.com

# Lesson 13

## Vocabulary

**gesture drawing**

**rhythm**

# Figures in Motion

**A** Edgar Degas, **Two Blue Dancers,** about 1900, pastel on paper, 75 cm × 49 cm. Von der Heydt Museum, Wuppertal, Germany.

**B** Edgar Degas, **Study of a Dancer (Etude de Danseuse),** pastel and charcoal on paper, $12\frac{3}{4}$ in. × $8\frac{1}{2}$ in.

Artists create portraits of people in still poses and of people in motion. What are the people in image **A** doing? How can you tell they are in motion?

## Gesture Drawing

Before artists create a finished artwork, they draw a sketch. Image **B** shows a sketch that Edgar Degas (duh•GAH) made of a ballerina. One kind of sketch, a **gesture drawing**, is created by using loose arm movements. Why do you think an artist might use a gesture drawing to sketch a person in motion?

98

# Rhythm

In music, when a sound is repeated, it creates a beat or rhythm. Artists create a visual beat or **rhythm** by repeating lines, shapes, or colors. Both artists and musicians may use rhythm to create a certain mood. Look at images **A** and **B**. How do the lines of the arms show rhythm?

Lyonel Feininger, the artist of image **C**, was trained as a violinist before he became an artist. How do you think his training as a musician may have helped him as an artist? How did he create rhythm in image **C**? What kind of feeling did he show?

**LOCATE IT**

The painting in image **C** can be found at the National Gallery of Art in Washington, D.C.

**Washington, D.C.**

**See Maps of Museums and Art Sites, pages 206–209.**

**Lyonel Feininger, *The Bicycle Race,***
1912, oil on canvas, 31$\frac{5}{8}$ in. × 39$\frac{1}{2}$ in.
**National Gallery of Art, Washington, D.C.**

Read the title of image D. Do you think this is a good title for the painting? Why or why not? How did the artist of image D use rhythm?

## Think Critically

1. **READING SKILL** What are the characters, setting, and plot in image C? **NARRATIVE ELEMENTS**

2. How would you change the shapes in image C to show a different feeling?

3. **WRITE** Look at image D. Write a story about why the child was running on the balcony.

 **Giacomo Balla,** *Child Who Runs on the Balcony,* 1912, oil on canvas, 127.5 cm × 127.5 cm. Civica Galleria d'Arte Moderna, Milan, Italy.

# Artist's Workshop

## Create a Panel Drawing

**MATERIALS**

- pencil
- sketchbook
- white paper
- crayons

**PLAN**

Brainstorm a list of steps for performing an action, such as hitting a baseball. Then have a partner model the steps. Use simple lines and shapes to make gesture drawings of your partner.

**CREATE**

1. Fold a sheet of paper into three sections, or panels. Draw a vertical line along each fold to separate the sections.

2. Use your gesture drawings as a guide to draw your subject at the beginning, middle, and end of the action. Make a drawing in each panel.

3. Use crayons to add color and details to your panel drawing.

**REFLECT**

What kind of action did you show in your panel drawing? If you cut your panel drawing apart, could your partner put the panels back in order?

**Quick Tip**

For help with drawing figures in motion, look back at page 98.

# Relief Sculpture

Have you ever reached into your pocket and felt the raised surface of a coin? The people and symbols on our coins are shown as relief sculptures. A **relief sculpture** is an image that stands out from the background surface. Image **A** is a relief sculpture of Lewis and Clark's Native American guide, Sacagawea.

 Glenna Goodacre and Thomas Rogers, Sacagawea coin, designed in 1999.

## Subtractive Method

To make relief sculptures, artists may carve a slab of material such as clay or marble. This process is called the **subtractive method** because the artist cuts away, or subtracts, some of the original material.

**B** Gutzon Borglum, *Mount Rushmore National Memorial,* 1927–1941, granite, 60 ft. high. Near Rapid City, South Dakota.

Image **B** shows a huge relief sculpture on the side of a mountain. Gutzon Borglum created this sculpture of four United States Presidents—George Washington, Thomas Jefferson, Theodore Roosevelt, and Abraham Lincoln. Most sculptors use small, handheld tools for carving, but Borglum used dynamite and huge drills.

**C** Unknown artist, *Embarkation on Ship of Roman Troops,* (detail from Trajan's Column), about A.D. 106–113, marble. Rome, Italy.

## Positive and Negative Space

Relief sculptures have both positive space and negative space. The raised areas make up the **positive space**. The **negative space** is where the artist cut away the original material to create the raised areas. Look at image **C**. What objects are shown in the positive space?

**103**

**LOCATE IT**

The artwork in image **D** can be found in southern Egypt.

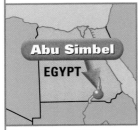

See Maps of Museums and Art Sites, pages 206–209.

# Relief Sculptures in History

Throughout history, relief sculptures have been used to show leaders and to record historical or cultural events. Image **D** shows a relief sculpture of the ancient Egyptian ruler Ramses II. This sculpture was carved into a sandstone wall at the entrance of a temple in Egypt.

Image **E** shows a twentieth-century relief sculpture from the Texas State History Museum. It celebrates Neil Armstrong's historic first step on the moon. How did the sculptor of this artwork use positive and negative space?

 Unknown artist, **Head of Colossus of Ramses II,** about 1250 B.C., sandstone. Abu Simbel, Egypt.

 Mike O'Brien, *Moon Landing,* 2001, glass fiber reinforced concrete, 11 ft. × 16 ft. The Bob Bullock Texas State History Museum, Austin, Texas.

## Think Critically

1. **READING SKILL** What is the setting of the scene in image **C**? **NARRATIVE ELEMENTS**

2. Why is the process of carving called the subtractive method?

3. **WRITE** Describe an event you would like to show in a relief sculpture.

# Artist's Workshop

## Carve a Relief Sculpture

**MATERIALS**

- pencil
- sketchbook
- clay
- plastic knife
- sharpened pencil or paper clip
- craft stick

### PLAN

Choose a friend or classmate whose portrait you would like to create. Sketch a portrait of your friend's face.

### CREATE

1. Flatten a slab of clay. Then trim the edges with a plastic knife to form a background for your relief sculpture.

2. Use a pencil point to carve the outline of your portrait. Use a craft stick or other carving tool to carve away clay to create negative space.

3. Use a pencil point or one end of an opened paper clip to carve details into the clay.

### REFLECT

Point out the positive space and negative space in your relief sculpture.

**Safety Tips**

Use tools one at a time. Remember to point sharp objects away from your body.

# Marisol Escobar

*How might an artist represent herself and others in an artwork?*

**Marisol, *President Charles DeGaulle*,** 1967, wood, plaster, and mirror, $107\frac{1}{4}$ in. x $86\frac{1}{4}$ in. x $31\frac{7}{8}$ in. Smithsonian American Art Museum, Washington, D.C.

**A**s a young girl, Marisol Escobar dreamed of becoming an artist. She first studied art at the age of sixteen, hoping to become a painter. Encouraged by her father, she later studied in Paris and New York.

As Marisol studied art and met other artists, she learned about other ways of expressing herself, besides painting. She began to experiment with clay and wood carving, which she combined in her artwork.

Marisol, who decided to use just her first name, became known for her witty, large wooden figures. She painted the figures and attached everyday objects and pieces of her own clothing to them. She sometimes included plaster casts of her own face, hands, and feet. Marisol's artwork often expressed her feelings about herself and the world around her in a humorous way.

Marisol has created many sculptures of friends, world leaders, and famous artists. Look at images **A** and **B**. What objects in the sculptures surprise you? How do you think the artist feels about the subjects of these artworks?

## DID YOU KNOW?

**M**arisol's sculpture *The Generals* shows George Washington and Simón Bolívar on a horse. This artwork contains a built-in phonograph that plays military music. Bolívar is known as the George Washington of South America. He led several revolutions against Spanish rule and became president of Colombia and of Peru.

**B** Marisol, *The Generals*, 1961–1962, wood and mixed media, 87 in. x 28 in. x 76 in. Albright-Knox Art Gallery, Buffalo, New York.

## Think About Art

Think of a person you admire. If Marisol created a sculpture of that person, what objects might she include?

**GO** ONLINE **Multimedia Biographies** Visit *The Learning Site* www.harcourtschool.com

# Sculpture in History

A sculpture is an example of a **form**. A form is a three-dimensional shape. It has length, width, and height. One type of sculpture is a statue. A statue takes up positive space. It is surrounded on all sides by negative space.

## Ancient Statues

Look at image **A**, which shows a statue of a boy. What does the boy's clothing tell you about when or where he lived? The ancient Greeks and Romans carved detailed statues, with lifelike proportions, out of marble. They used the subtractive method to shape blocks of marble into portraits of their leaders and other important people.

**A** Unknown artist, *Neron Child,* marble. The Louvre Museum, Paris, France.

Image **B** shows a statue from ancient China. In the third century B.C., the first Chinese emperor wanted to be buried with an army of soldiers to protect him after he died. Thousands of statues like this one were sculpted in terra-cotta. **Terra-cotta** is a kind of reddish brown clay that sculptors shape with their hands and then bake until it hardens.

The Chinese statues have different designs on their uniforms and armor. These designs show each soldier's rank. The emperor's artists also sculpted horses, chariots, and weapons for the soldiers. Archaeologists are still uncovering this army of statues to learn more about this ancient Chinese civilization.

**B** Unknown artist, *Terra-Cotta Army Figure,* about 210 B.C. Warrior tomb of Qin Shi Huangdi, Xi´an, China.

## LOCATE IT

The original version of the artwork in image C can be found at the Amon Carter Museum in Fort Worth, Texas.

TEXAS

Fort Worth

See Maps of Museums and Art Sites, pages 206–209.

# Modern Materials

Over time, sculptors began to use materials other than stone and clay for their art. The sculptures shown in images C and D were made in the twentieth century. They are made of bronze, a kind of metal.

Do the subjects of image C seem to be in motion? What parts of the sculpture give the sense that the subjects are moving?

**C** Frederic Remington, *The Rattlesnake,* 1905, bronze reproduction, $22\frac{5}{8}$ in. × 13 in. Buffalo Bill Historical Center, Cody, Wyoming.

**D** Man Ray, *Man Ray,* 1971, painted bronze and plexiglass, 8 in. high without base.

## Think Critically

1. **READING SKILL** What do you think the characters, setting, and plot are in image C? **NARRATIVE ELEMENTS**

2. What are some differences between the ancient and modern statues shown in this lesson?

3. **WRITE** Write a short story about the statue in image B. Include characters, setting, and plot.

# Artist's Workshop

## Carve a Soap Sculpture

**MATERIALS**

- magazines or newspapers
- newsprint
- bar of soap
- toothpick or paper clip
- plastic knife
- scrubber sponge

**PLAN**

Find a magazine or newspaper photograph of an animal you would like to sculpt.

**CREATE**

1. Place a bar of soap on a sheet of newsprint. Use a toothpick or the end of a paper clip to carve the outline of your animal on both sides of the soap.

2. Use a plastic knife to shave away the soap around the outline.

3. When you are finished, use a scrubber sponge to smooth the surface of the sculpture.

**REFLECT**

What kind of animal did you sculpt? How did you use the subtractive method?

**Quick Tip**

Try not to cut away big pieces of the soap all at once. Work slowly, carving a little at a time.

**111**

# Unit 3 Review and Reflect

## Vocabulary and Concepts

**Choose the letter of the word or phrase that best completes each sentence.**

1 Artworks that artists create of themselves are ___.

   **A** self-portraits    **C** patterns

   **B** portraits    **D** forms

2 ___ is a type of abstract art.

   **F** Terra-cotta    **H** Form

   **G** Cubism    **J** Rhythm

3 ___ is the visual beat created by repeated lines and shapes.

   **A** Abstract art    **C** Rhythm

   **B** Color    **D** Space

4 In a relief sculpture, the raised area is called ___ space.

   **F** abstract    **H** rhythm

   **G** positive    **J** negative

5 A ___ is a three-dimensional shape.

   **A** pattern    **C** distortion

   **B** form    **D** terra-cotta

## Focus Skill READING SKILL

### Narrative Elements

**Select an artwork in this unit, and write a story about it. Trade stories with a partner. Use a diagram like this to record the narrative elements in your partner's story.**

| Characters | Setting |
|---|---|

| Plot (Story Events) |
|---|
| 1. |
| 2. |
| 3. |

## Write About Art

Choose a piece of your own artwork, and write a story about it. Describe the characters, setting, and events in the plot. Use a diagram like the one on page 112 to help you plan your writing.

### REMEMBER — YOU SHOULD

- use descriptive words that make your story interesting.

- use correct grammar, spelling, and punctuation.

## Critic's Corner

**Look at *Golconda* by René Magritte to answer the questions below.**

**René Magritte, *Golconda,***
1953, oil on canvas, 31$\frac{5}{8}$ in. × 39$\frac{3}{8}$ in.
Menil Foundation, Houston, Texas.

**DESCRIBE** What do you think are the characters, setting, and plot in the artwork?

**ANALYZE** How has the artist created rhythm in this artwork?

**INTERPRET** What ideas do you think the artist expressed in this artwork?

**EVALUATE** What is your opinion of the story this artwork tells?

Faith Ringgold, *The Sunflower Quilting Bee at Arles,*
1996, color lithograph, 22 in. × 30 in.

## LOCATE IT

This painting can be found at the Philadelphia Museum
of Art in Philadelphia, Pennsylvania.

**See Maps of Museums and Art Sites, pages 206–209.**

PENNSYLVANIA

Philadelphia

# Art Reflects Culture

## Step into the Art

Imagine that you could step into this artwork and join the women holding the quilt. What might they be talking about? What would you ask them? The man on the right side of the image is the artist Vincent van Gogh. What would you say to him?

## Unit Vocabulary

| | | |
|---|---|---|
| weaving | symmetrical balance | visual weight |
| pattern | radial balance | folk art |
| tapestry | asymmetrical balance | symbols |
| vertical axis | | |

### ABOUT THE ARTIST

See Gallery of Artists, pages 240–253.

**GO** ONLINE

Multimedia Art Glossary
Visit *The Learning Site*
www.harcourtschool.com

# Compare and Contrast

**When you think about how things are alike, you *compare*.**
**When you think about how things are different, you *contrast*.**

Look at the objects shown below. They are **alike** in these ways:

• Both are pieces of clothing with long sleeves.

• Both have designs on them.

They are **different** in these ways:

• Image **A** has organic shapes in its design. Image **B** has geometric shapes in its design.

• Image **B** has fringe, and image **A** does not.

**A** **Unknown artist, British herald's tunic,** 1707–1714, silk, metallic thread, beads, back length 34 in. Philadelphia Museum of Art, Philadelphia, Pennsylvania.

**B** **Unknown artist, Indian warrior's shirt,** buckskin with beadwork and fringe, 30 in. vertical.

Comparing and contrasting can help you understand what you read. Read this passage to learn more about the clothing in images **A** and **B**.

Eighteenth-century British soldiers and royalty decorated their garments, or clothing, with specific designs so that others could recognize them quickly. The Plains Indians of North America decorated their clothing with colorful geometric shapes that told about their tribes. The British garments were made of silk. The Indians used animal hides and glass beads to make their garments.

Compare and contrast the two types of garments. You can use a Venn diagram like this to help you.

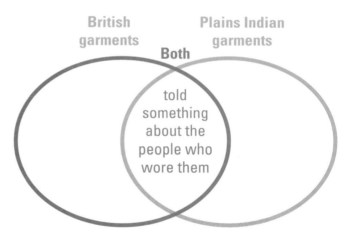

British garments

Plains Indian garments

**Both**

told something about the people who wore them

# On Your Own

As you read the lessons in this unit, use Venn diagrams to compare and contrast information that you read and artworks that you see. Look back at your diagrams when you see questions with Focus Skill *READING SKILL*.

# Fiber Art

An artist can choose from a variety of materials to create an artwork. Some artworks are made of fiber. Fibers are interlaced, or woven together, to create a **weaving**, or cloth.

## Patterns in Weavings

Look at the weavings in images **A** and **B**. What kinds of lines, shapes, and colors do you see in each one? When lines, shapes, or colors are repeated, they create a **pattern**. How are the patterns in images **A** and **B** alike? How are they different?

   The kente cloth in image **B** was made in Africa. The word *kente* comes from the word *kenten*, which means "basket." Notice that the pattern in the cloth looks like the pattern in a basket.

**A** **Unknown artist, Navajo traditional shawl,** about 1850–1860, wool, 59 in. × 43 in. Collection of the Lowe Art Museum, The University of Miami, Coral Gables, Florida.

**B** **Unknown artist, Detail of African kente cloth,** about mid-1900s, woven silk. The British Museum, London, England.

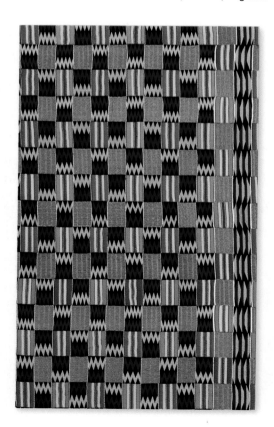

C ▶ **Unknown artist, Chinese Emperor's Twelve Symbol Robe,** Ch'ing dynasty (1644–1911), silk K'o-ssu tapestry weave, 58½ in. × 65 in. Collection of the Lowe Art Museum, The University of Miami, Coral Gables, Florida.

The robe in image C is an example of tapestry from China. A **tapestry** is a type of weaving that has colorful designs or scenes in it. Many tapestries are heavy and are hung on walls. Some are used in clothing. How is this robe like other robes you have seen? How is it different?

Social Studies Link

Long ago, kente cloth, such as that shown in image B, was worn by kings and other powerful people in Ghana, Africa.

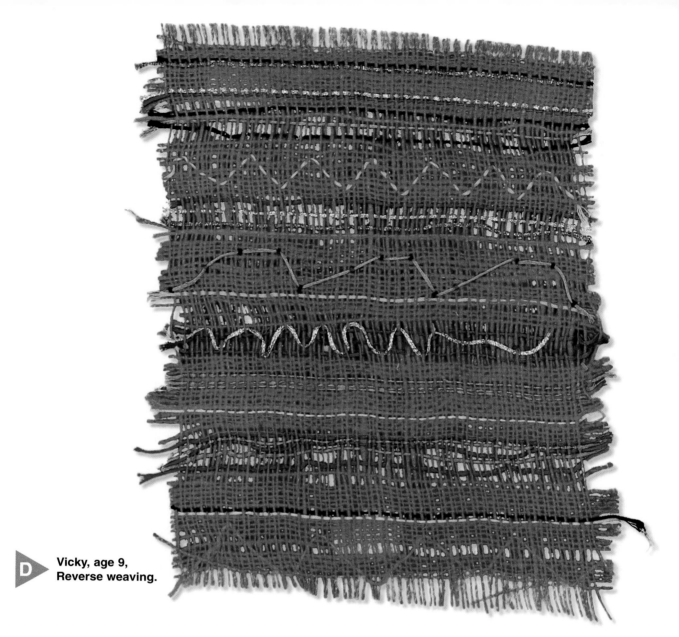

**D** Vicky, age 9,
Reverse weaving.

What kinds of patterns do you see in image **D**? Compare
image **D** with image **B**. How are the weavings alike? How
are they different?

## Think Critically

1. **Focus Skill** *READING SKILL* How are the weavings in images **A**
   and **D** alike and different? COMPARE AND CONTRAST

2. Describe the patterns you see in image **C**.

3. **WRITE** Write a paragraph describing a piece of
   clothing that is special to you. Include details about
   its color, pattern, or texture.

# Artist's Workshop

## Create a Reverse Weaving

PLAN

Look at the reverse weaving in image **D**. Think about the colors and patterns you would like to use in your own reverse weaving.

CREATE

1. Pull some of the strands out of a piece of burlap, creating open areas.

2. Measure and cut several pieces of yarn about an inch or so longer than the width of the burlap. Weave the yarn in and out of the strands of burlap.

3. After weaving several pieces of yarn, pinch the pieces together to create a tighter weave.

REFLECT

Describe the pattern you created in your weaving.

**MATERIALS**

- 6 in. × 6 in. burlap pieces
- colored yarn
- ruler
- scissors

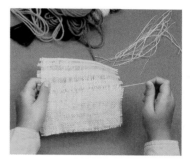

**Quick Tip**

Tape one end of the yarn to the tip of a craft stick. Use the craft stick like a needle to weave through the burlap.

121

# Balance in Masks

Almost every culture in the world has created masks for special events and celebrations.

## Symmetrical Balance

Image **A** shows a mask from the Aztec culture. Hundreds of years ago, the Aztecs ruled a large part of what is now central and southern Mexico.

Use your finger to trace a line down the middle of image **A**. This line is the **vertical axis** of the artwork. Compare the left side of the mask to the right side. The artist matched the lines and shapes on one side of the mask to those on the other side. Artworks with this kind of arrangement show **symmetrical balance**.

**A** Unknown artist, Aztec mask, about 1500, white jade, 10.5 cm × 14.5 cm × 4 cm. Peabody Museum, Harvard University, Cambridge, Massachusetts.

**Unknown artist, African Kwele mask,** pigment on carved wood, 26 in. high. Western Equatorial Africa.

## Materials in Masks

Ancient mask makers used materials such as tree bark, shells, minerals, leather, metals, wood, cornhusks, and feathers in their work.

Look at the African mask in image **B**. It was carved from wood. The mask in image **A** was carved from jade, a mineral that is usually green or white in color. Jade was used by the Aztecs and other ancient peoples to make jewelry and other decorative objects. How are the African mask and the Aztec mask alike? How are they different?

The name *Inuit* means "the people." Today, there are more than 100,000 Inuits living in a region that stretches from Greenland in the west to eastern Siberia.

C ► Unknown artist, **Inuit finger masks,** 19th century, carved wood, $4\frac{1}{2}$ in. × $3\frac{1}{8}$ in. × $\frac{5}{8}$ in. The Detroit Institute of Arts, Detroit, Michigan.

## Finger Masks

The masks in image **C** were not worn on the face. Inuit women wore one of these finger masks on each hand. They danced with their hands and kept their feet still. Do the masks in image **C** show symmetrical balance? How do you know?

Compare the masks in image **C** to the mask in image **D**. How are they alike? How are they different?

D ▼ Caleb, age 9, Paper sculpture mask.

**Think Critically**

1. **READING SKILL** How is the mask in image **A** different from a human face? How is it the same? **COMPARE AND CONTRAST**

2. Does the mask in image **D** show symmetrical balance? Why or why not?

3. **WRITE** Imagine a party where people might wear masks. Write a paragraph about the party and the kinds of masks you might see there.

# Artist's Workshop

## Create a Paper Mask

**MATERIALS**

- pencil
- poster board
- scissors
- markers or paint
- paintbrushes
- glue
- colored paper
- decorative materials

**PLAN**

Sketch some ideas for a mask you would like to make. Use lines, shapes, and colors to create symmetrical balance.

**CREATE**

1. Choose your best sketch, and draw the outline of your mask on poster board.

2. Cut out your mask. Cut holes for eyes and other facial features.

3. Add color and other details to your mask with markers or paint, colored paper, feathers, or beads.

**REFLECT**

How does your mask show symmetrical balance? What kinds of materials did you use, and why did you choose them?

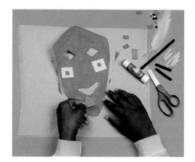

**Safety Tips**

Carefully poke a hole in the center of the area you want to remove. Cut the outline of the facial feature from that center point.

# AMEDEO MODIGLIANI

*How can an artist's work be influenced by the art of another culture?*

The painter and sculptor Amedeo Modigliani (moh•deel•YAH•nee) was born in Italy and studied art in Paris. He was surrounded by many famous artists whom he admired. At first, Modigliani's artwork looked like theirs, but then he worked to create his own style.

**A** Amedeo Modigliani, *Self-Portrait,* 1919, oil on canvas, 100 cm x 65 cm. Museum of Contemporary Art, University of São Paulo, São Paulo, Brazil

**B** Amedeo Modigliani, *Head of a Caryatid (Tête de Cariatide),* about 1910–1911, blue crayon on paper, 16 in. x 6⅝ in.

**C** Amedeo Modigliani, *Head (Tête),* about 1911–1912, stone.

Look at the self-portrait in image **A**. Compare it to the other images on these pages. How are images **A**, **B**, **C**, and **D** alike?

How would you describe the style of Modigliani's artwork? Look back at the African mask on page 123. How is it like Modigliani's work? How is it different?

Modigliani studied different styles and artworks from outside Europe. Many artists in Paris became interested in African art at this time. Modigliani combined ideas from African masks and sculpture with European styles of carving to create something new.

# THINK ABOUT ART

Why do you think it is important to study art from other cultures?

 **D** **Amedeo Modigliani,**
*Jeanne Hebuterne,*
1917–1918, oil on canvas,
18 in. x 11 in.

## DID YOU KNOW?

**M**any artists use their family members and friends as models for their artwork. Modigliani's friend, Jeanne, was the model for the portrait in image **D**. Modigliani also painted portraits of the artists Diego Rivera and Pablo Picasso.

 **Multimedia Biographies**
Visit *The Learning Site*
www.harcourtschool.com

# Paper Art

The tradition of paper cutting came from ancient China. It is thought to have started about 206 B.C.—around the time that paper was invented. Eventually, the art of paper cutting spread to other parts of the world. Different cultures developed their own styles of paper cutting.

How did the artist of image **A** use shape to create symmetrical balance? What kinds of patterns do you see?

**A** Unknown artist, *Window Flowers for New Year,* about 1950, Chinese paper cutting, $8\frac{1}{2}$ in. × $4\frac{1}{2}$ in. Museum of International Folk Art/Museum of New Mexico, Santa Fe, New Mexico.

**B**

**Bernadine Jendrzejczak,
Paper cutting in Polish
traditional style,**
1998, cut paper on
white cardboard, 10 in.
Private collection.

Now look at image **B**. What shapes do you recognize? In
Poland it has been a tradition to make cutouts like this as
decorations for everyday use and for special occasions. The
patterns are often inspired by nature. Describe how image **B**
shows symmetrical balance.

Image **B** also shows **radial balance** because the same
pattern radiates, or extends, from the center, like the spokes
of a wheel. Put your finger on the center of image **B**. Then
look at the way the pattern is repeated around the artwork.

**129**

Image **C** shows an example of *papel picado*, which means "punched paper" in Spanish. In this traditional Mexican artwork, stacks of about fifty sheets of tissue paper are cut at one time with a small, sharp chisel. Designs might include people, animals, flowers, or words.

**C** ▶ Carmen Lomas Garza, *Flowery Words: Stories, Poems, Song, History & Wisdom,* 1993, white paper cutouts. Collection of the artist.

Trace the vertical axis in image **C**. This artwork shows **asymmetrical balance**. The artist arranged lines and shapes to show balance even though the artwork is not the same on both sides. Look at the woman's head in the lower right corner. Now look at the thick, curved line of the plant in the upper left corner. These two objects have the same **visual weight**, or importance, in the artwork. Artists use visual weight to create a sense of balance in their artworks.

## Think Critically

1. **(Focus Skill) READING SKILL** Compare the three artworks in this lesson. How are they alike? How are they different? **COMPARE AND CONTRAST**

2. How would you change image **C** to show symmetrical balance?

3. **WRITE** Write a paragraph to explain how you think the title of image **C** relates to the artwork.

# Artist's Workshop

## Create a Paper Cutting

**MATERIALS**

- pencil
- sketchbook
- white paper
- scissors
- colored pencils or markers

**PLAN**

Think of a design you would like to show in a paper cutting. Sketch some of your ideas.

**CREATE**

1. Fold a sheet of paper in half. Draw half of your design so that it meets the fold of the paper. Make your drawing large enough to fill up the folded paper.

2. Cut out your design. Then open the paper.

3. Add color with colored pencils or markers to the side of your design that does not have pencil marks.

**REFLECT**

How would you describe your paper cutting? What kind of balance does your design show?

**Quick Tip**

Do not cut all the way through the fold of your paper.

# Folk Art

Look at the scene shown in image **A**. How would you describe it? Notice the objects on each side of the painting. The artist balanced the visual weight of the checkered house on the left side with the running horses and dog and the red barns on the right side. Does image **A** show symmetrical balance or asymmetrical balance?

**Grandma Moses, *The Old Checkered House,***
1944, oil on pressed wood, 24 in. × 43 in.
Seiji Togo Museum, Gekkoso, Japan.

 Pedro Figari,
*Creole Dance,*
oil on board,
19.75 cm x 27.5 cm.

The style of the artwork shown in this lesson is called folk art. **Folk art** is created by people who have had little formal training in art. Folk artists often use art techniques that have been passed down through their families or cultures. Most folk artists use materials that are easy for them to find. For example, instead of painting on a canvas, a folk artist might paint on a piece of wood.

Some folk artists create art to help people remember part of their culture. Look at image **B**. What kind of event do you think the artist was trying to show? Now look at the colors and shapes the artist used to make certain parts of the artwork stand out. Does this painting show symmetrical balance or asymmetrical balance? Why do you think so?

133

**LOCATE IT**

The artwork in image C can be found at the Philadelphia Museum of Art in Philadelphia, Pennsylvania.

**PENNSYLVANIA**

**Philadelphia**

**See Maps of Museums and Art Sites, pages 206–209.**

Look at image C. The artist created this sculpture from wood. How would you describe the kind of balance shown in this sculpture?

**C** Unknown artist, *Bird Tree,* about 1800–1830, painted hardwoods, wire, $17\frac{3}{8}$ in. high. Philadelphia Museum of Art, Philadelphia, Pennsylvania.

## Think Critically

1. **(Focus Skill) READING SKILL** Compare the settings in images A and B. How are they alike? How are they different?
   **COMPARE AND CONTRAST**

2. Which objects have the most visual weight in image C?

3. **WRITE** Write a short story describing the events in image A.

**134**

# Artist's Workshop

## Create a Folk Art Painting

**MATERIALS**

- pencil
- sketchbook
- white paper
- tempera paint
- paintbrushes
- water bowl

**PLAN**

Think of a tradition your family or community has that you would like to paint. Sketch some ideas. Think of ways to create asymmetrical balance in your painting.

**CREATE**

1. Choose your best sketch, and copy it onto white paper.

2. Before you begin to paint, make sure both sides of your drawing have the same visual weight.

3. Use tempera paint to finish your artwork.

**REFLECT**

What subject did you choose for your painting? How did you create asymmetrical balance?

**Quick Tip**

Remember that visual weight can be created with lines, shapes, or colors that make the artwork seem balanced.

# COWHANDS IN ART

*How do artists help us remember the lifestyle of the American cowhand?*

**A** **W. Herbert Dunton,** *Old Texas,*
1929, oil on canvas, 28 in. x 39 in. San Antonio
Art League Museum, San Antonio, Texas.

Cowhands have a special place in American culture. Their long journeys guiding cattle from Texas into the Great Plains of the United States were full of challenges. Their adventures have inspired imaginations all over the world since the first cattle drives of the 1800s. Artists created images that introduced the rest of the world to the cowhand's way of life.

136

**B** Richard Haas, *Cowgirl Mural* on the
east exterior wall of the National
Cowgirl Museum and Hall of Fame,
2002, Artex paint over sealant and primer,
22 ft. x 36 ft. Fort Worth, Texas.

Today, cowhands still live and work in
parts of the United States. Many things
have changed, but one important part of
the cowhand's life continues to thrill
Americans—the rodeo.

Rodeos began in the 1800s so that
cowhands could show off their skills in
riding horses and roping cattle. Today, rodeo
performers compete for prizes in front of
cheering crowds. Just like the cowhands of
the Old West, rodeo cowhands inspire artists.

# THINK
## ABOUT ART

Why do you think the life of a cowhand
was so inspiring to artists?

## DID YOU KNOW?

The National Cowgirl Museum and Hall
of Fame, in Fort Worth, Texas, honors the
lives of women who represented the
spirit of the American West. These
women include Narcissa Prentiss
Whitman, the first pioneer woman to
cross the Rockies, and Georgia O'Keeffe,
an artist who painted scenes of the
American Southwest.

National Cowgirl Museum and Hall of Fame

# Symbols in Art

**Symbols** are pictures or objects that stand for ideas. Artists may use symbols to communicate ideas and feelings through art. The artist of image **A** showed a Fourth of July celebration. What symbols did he use to express his feelings of patriotism? What kind of feeling do you get from image **A**?

 **Frederick Childe Hassam,** *The Fourth of July,* 1916, oil on canvas, 36 in. × 26 in.

Warren Kimble,
*The American Farm,*
2000, acrylic on antique
wood, 16½ in. × 23 in.
Private collection.

Different artists may convey the same message, such as patriotism, in different ways. Read the title of the painting in image **B**. The artist used his subject as a symbol. The American farm is a symbol of traditional rural life in the United States. How do you think the artist felt about rural life? What other symbols do you see in image **B**? Describe the patterns the artist created. How did he use these patterns as symbols?

A law written in 1993 states that the red and blue colors in the Texas state flag are to be the same as those in the United States flag. These colors are known as Old Glory Red and Old Glory Blue.

The artist of image **C** has put patriotic symbols together in a new way. What symbols do you recognize? What message do you think this artist is trying to convey? Does the artwork in image **C** show symmetrical balance or asymmetrical balance?

**C** Sante Graziani, *George Washington,* 1968, woodcut print, 12 in. × 12 in. Private collection.

## Think Critically

1. **READING SKILL** Compare and contrast the patterns you see in images **A** and **B**. **COMPARE AND CONTRAST**

2. What other symbols can you think of that can give a message of patriotism or state pride?

3. **WRITE** Look at image **C**. Write a paragraph describing what the symbols in this artwork mean to you.

# Create a Print

**MATERIALS**

- pencil
- sketchbook
- foam tray
- tempera paint
- foam brush
- water bowl
- white or colored paper

**PLAN**

**Think of a design for a rubber stamp that shows symbols. Make some sketches.**

**CREATE**

1. **Choose your best sketch, and draw it lightly onto a foam tray. Carve your drawing into the foam by pressing with a dull pencil point.**

2. **Spread a thin layer of tempera paint evenly over the foam tray with a foam brush.**

3. **Lay a clean sheet of paper across the wet paint. Press gently and evenly on the paper with your fingers. Then carefully lift the paper off the tray.**

**REFLECT**

**What does the symbol in your print mean to you?**

Quick Tip

You can use the foam tray again by rinsing off the paint. Apply another color of paint to the tray to make a different print.

141

# Unit 4 Review and Reflect

## Vocabulary and Concepts

**Choose the letter of the word or phrase that best completes each sentence.**

**1** Repeated lines, shapes, or colors create a ___.

  **A** weaving     **C** tapestry

  **B** pattern     **D** symbol

**2** An artwork shows ___ when both sides are the same.

  **F** pattern     **H** asymmetrical balance

  **G** symbols     **J** symmetrical balance

**3** An artwork shows ___ when the same patterns extend from its center.

  **A** radial balance     **C** depth

  **B** asymmetrical balance     **D** symbols

**4** Artists may use ___ to create a sense of balance.

  **F** pattern     **H** visual weight

  **G** tapestry     **J** symbols

**5** A ___ is a picture or object that stands for an idea.

  **A** pattern     **C** tapestry

  **B** weaving     **D** symbol

## Focus Skill — READING SKILL

### Compare and Contrast

Select two artworks from different lessons in this unit, and reread the information about them. Use a Venn diagram to compare and contrast them.

Artwork 1    Both    Artwork 2

## Write About Art

**Choose two pieces of your own artwork, and write a composition in which you compare and contrast them. Use a Venn diagram to plan your writing. Use unit vocabulary words to describe each artwork.**

### REMEMBER — YOU SHOULD

- write about the similarities in one paragraph and the differences in another.
- use correct grammar, spelling, and punctuation.

## Critic's Corner

**Look at *Four Seasons* by John Biggers to answer the questions below.**

**DESCRIBE** What are the subjects in the artwork? How would you describe them? How are the figures in the artwork alike? How are they different?

**John Biggers,** *Four Seasons,*
**1984, color lithograph, 24 in. × 32 in.
Private collection.**

**ANALYZE** Does the artwork show symmetrical balance or asymmetrical balance?

**INTERPRET** What ideas do you think the artist was trying to express in this artwork?

**EVALUATE** What is your opinion of the way the artist showed the four seasons in this artwork?

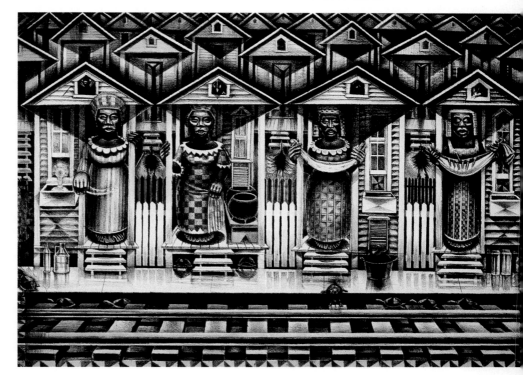

143

Gustave Caillebotte, *Paris Street, Rainy Day*,
1877, oil on canvas, 212.2 cm × 276.2 cm.

**LOCATE IT**

This painting can be found at the Art Institute
of Chicago in Chicago, Illinois.

**See Maps of Museums and Art Sites, pages 206–209.**

Chicago

ILLINOIS

144

# The Artist's Environment

## Step into the Art

Imagine you could step into the scene in this painting. Describe what you would hear and feel. Which person would you talk to? What would you say to that person?

## ABOUT THE ARTIST

See Gallery of Artists, pages 240–253.

## Unit Vocabulary

| | | |
|---|---|---|
| space | atmospheric perspective | movement |
| depth | horizon line | unity |
| foreground | | architect |
| background | linear perspective | mural |
| middle ground | vanishing point | trompe l'oeil |

**Multimedia Art Glossary**
Visit *The Learning Site*
www.harcourtschool.com

# Summarize and Paraphrase

When you *summarize*, you tell only main ideas or important events. When you *paraphrase*, you use your own words to restate information or to retell a story. When you paraphrase, you give more details than when you summarize.

Look at the image below. You can **summarize** the image like this:

• People are enjoying an outdoor swimming pool in different ways.

You can **paraphrase** the image like this:

• Many people have come to the swimming pool to enjoy the day. Some are talking, some are resting, and others are looking at the water.

**William James Glackens,** *Outdoor Swimming Pool,*
oil on canvas, 18 in. × 24 in.

To make sure that you understand what you read, you can summarize or paraphrase the text. Read this passage:

Lara spent the whole day at the community swimming pool. She saw a lot of people there. Most of them were sunbathing at the edge of the pool, but a few people were getting ready to swim. A little boy and his mother sat on the ground, playing with some toys. Two women sat on a bench, talking and laughing. Everyone seemed to be enjoying the day.

Summarize the passage in two sentences. Then paraphrase the passage in a new paragraph. You can use a chart like this to help you.

| Summary: Main Ideas Only |
| --- |
| Lara spent the whole day at the pool. She saw a lot of people having fun in different ways. |
| **Paraphrase: Main Ideas and Details in Your Own Words** |
| |

# On Your Own

As you read the lessons in this unit, use charts like the one above to summarize and paraphrase when you read information and view artworks. Look back at your charts when you see questions with (Focus Skill) *READING SKILL* .

# Depth and Distance

## Vocabulary

space

depth

foreground

background

middle ground

**Space** is the three-dimensional area around, between, and within objects. One way an artist can show space on a flat surface is to create the feeling of depth. **Depth** is the appearance of space or distance in an artwork. Artists use different techniques to show depth.

## Foreground, Middle Ground, and Background

Look at image **A**. The artist created a feeling of depth by dividing the scene into parts. The part that seems closest to the viewer is called the **foreground**. The part that seems farthest from the viewer is called the **background**. The part that is between the foreground and the background is called the **middle ground**. What do you see in the foreground of image **A**? What do you see in the middle ground and background?

**A** Jean Baptiste Camille Corot, *Marcoussis— Cows Grazing,* 1845–1850, oil on canvas, $16\frac{1}{4}$ in. × $29\frac{5}{8}$ in. Private Collection.

**LOCATE IT**

The artwork shown in image **B** can be found in the Netherlands.

**THE NETHERLANDS**

Otterlo

See Maps of Museums and Art Sites, pages 206–209.

**B** Vincent van Gogh, *Café Terrace on the Place du Forum, Arles, At Night,* 1888, oil on canvas, 81 cm × 65.5 cm. Kröller-Müller Museum, Otterlo, the Netherlands.

## Detail and Distance

Now look at the scene in image **B**. What do you see in the foreground? The artist used thick, curved lines to paint the cobblestones in this part of the street. Notice how much less detail the artist used to paint the cobblestones in the background. Objects that have more detail seem to be closer to the viewer. Objects that have less detail seem to be farther away.

## Size and Distance

What do you notice about the sizes of the trees in image C?
Larger objects seem to be closer to the viewer. Smaller
objects seem to be farther away. Compare the trees in the
foreground to those in the background. How did the artist
use detail to show distance?

 **Jack Gunter, *The Discovery,***
2001, oil on canvas, 78 in. × 42 in.
Private collection.

## Think Critically

1. **READING SKILL** Summarize what you think the artist's
   message is in image A. **SUMMARIZE AND PARAPHRASE**

2. How did the artist use size to show depth in image A?

3. **WRITE** Read the title of image C. Write a short story
   telling about the discovery.

# Artist's Workshop

## Create Depth in a Scene

**MATERIALS**

- pencil
- sketchbook
- white paper
- oil pastels

**PLAN**

Think of an outdoor scene you would like to draw. Sketch some ideas. Think about how you can show depth in your scene by changing the sizes or details of the objects you draw.

**CREATE**

1. Choose your best sketch, and copy it onto white paper.

2. Use oil pastels to add color to your drawing.

**REFLECT**

How did you show depth in your drawing? What did you draw in the foreground, middle ground, and background?

**Quick Tip**

You may want to look through books and magazines for ideas for your drawing.

# Perspective Techniques

## Atmospheric Perspective

Artists use different perspective techniques to create the feeling of depth and distance in flat artworks. Look at the background in image **A**. The artist used a technique called **atmospheric perspective** to create the feeling of great distance. He used dull colors and fuzzy edges to make objects seem to fade away in the distance.

 Albert Bierstadt, *Among the Sierra Nevada Mountains, California,* 1868, oil on canvas, 183 cm × 305 cm. National Museum of American Art, Washington, D.C.

## Horizon Line

Find the place in image **B** where the sky seems to meet the land. This is called the **horizon line**. In image **B** the horizon line appears high up in the scene. The artist was probably sitting down and looking up when he painted the artwork. Where do you think the horizon line would be if the artist had been standing as he painted?

# Linear Perspective

Imagine you are standing on the walkway in image **C** and looking into the distance. Does the walkway seem to get wider or narrower in the distance? The artist of image **C** used **linear perspective** to show depth. He made the lines of the walkway get closer together until they reached the horizon line. The point where these lines seem to meet the horizon line is called the **vanishing point**. Where else do you see lines that meet at a vanishing point?

**C** Don Jacot, *Commuter Trains, Union Station,* 1991, oil on linen, 36 in. × 48 in. Louis K. Meisel Gallery, New York, New York.

## Think Critically

1. **READING SKILL** Summarize the technique of linear perspective. **SUMMARIZE AND PARAPHRASE**

2. Why do artists use a vanishing point?

3. **WRITE** Imagine you are riding one of the trains in image **C**. Write a paragraph telling where you are going and what you will do when you arrive.

# Artist's Workshop

## Draw a Scene with Linear Perspective

**MATERIALS**

- pencil
- sketchbook
- white paper
- ruler
- colored pencils

**PLAN**

Brainstorm some ways to show linear perspective in a scene. You might show the lines in a road, a path, or train tracks come together at a vanishing point.

**CREATE**

1. Sketch your scene on white paper. Use a ruler to draw the lines to the vanishing point.

2. Experiment with the sizes of objects to create the feeling of depth in your drawing.

3. Finish your drawing with colored pencils.

**REFLECT**

How did you use linear perspective in your drawing? What other ways did you use to show depth?

**Quick Tip**

Think of drawing a large upside-down *V* for *vanishing point.*

# MISSION ARCHITECTURE

*How can building styles show different ways of life?*

In the late 1600s and early 1700s, the Spanish were eager to expand their territory in the New World. They began building settlements called missions in what are now Texas, New Mexico, and California.

The missions of the American Southwest were designed to meet the needs of the people who lived there. They were often surrounded by walls for protection. Inside the walls were houses, workplaces, a school, and a church. Outside the walls, the settlers raised crops and tended livestock. The missions were built to be self-sufficient. This means that everything the people needed was produced at the mission.

**A** **San Francisco de Asis Mission,**
Taos, New Mexico.

**B** Mission Nuestra Señora de la Concepción de Acuña, San Antonio, Texas.

Image **A** is a photograph of a mission built in New Mexico. The walls of the mission were built with adobe (uh•DOH•bee), a kind of brick made from mud and chopped straw. Adobe is often used in areas with hot, dry weather. An adobe building stays cool in the summer and warm in the winter. Adobe is still used throughout the southwestern United States.

Image **B** shows a mission in San Antonio, Texas. How is it different from the mission in image **A**?

# THINK ABOUT ART

Why are building styles different in different locations?

157

# Garden Design

Look at image **A**. The designer arranged the lines in the garden to show **movement**, or to guide the viewer's eyes from place to place. As you look at image **A**, think about the way your eyes move along the diagonal lines.

Now look at the different parts of the garden. This garden design shows unity. **Unity** is a sense of completeness in an artwork. An artwork has unity when its parts fit together well.

 **Garden at Villandry, France.**

**Flower Conservatory,
Golden Gate Park,**
San Francisco, California.

Landscape designers choose color schemes for their
gardens. How would you describe the color scheme shown
in image **B**? Does the garden have symmetrical balance or
asymmetrical balance? How did the designer give this
garden a sense of unity?

**LOCATE IT**

The garden in image C is located in Brooklyn, New York.

**See Maps of Museums and Art Sites, pages 206–209.**

Desert Pavilion at the Brooklyn
Botanical Garden,
Brooklyn, New York.

Now look at image **C**. What kinds of plants do you see in this garden? What textures do these plants have? The designer of this garden used plants with similar textures and colors to create a sense of unity.

## Think Critically

1. **READING SKILL** Summarize what you learned about unity in one or two sentences. **SUMMARIZE AND PARAPHRASE**

2. What kind of balance is shown in image **C**? How do you know?

3. **WRITE** Which one of the gardens shown in this lesson would you most like to visit? Write a paragraph describing what you might see, smell, and feel if you visited that garden.

# Artist's Workshop

## Design a Park

**MATERIALS**

- pencil
- sketchbook
- colored pencils or markers
- magazines
- scissors
- glue

**PLAN**

Imagine a park where you would enjoy spending time. Think about the kinds of trees, plants, rocks, and other objects you would like in your park. Sketch your ideas.

**CREATE**

1. Use your sketches as a guide to draw your park design on white paper. Arrange the parts of your design in a way that shows movement.

2. Choose a color scheme for the plants and other objects in your park.

3. Find magazine pictures with colors and textures you like. Cut them out, and glue them onto your drawing.

**REFLECT**

How does your drawing show unity? What would you name your park?

**Quick Tip**

You may want to include such things as ponds, benches, statues, or fountains to make your park more interesting.

# Architectural Balance

An **architect** is a person who designs buildings. Architects design houses, churches, and schools. They design skyscrapers for large cities. Skyscrapers were developed in the late nineteenth century in the United States because of the growing population of the cities. Land was expensive, so tall buildings were built on small pieces of land. Today we see skyscrapers in almost every major city in the world.

Look at the skyscraper in image **A**. Does this building have symmetrical balance or asymmetrical balance? How do you know?

**Chase Building,**
Dallas, Texas.

 **Norman Foster,
City Hall,
London, England.**

Have you ever seen a building like the one in image **B**? How would you describe it? Move your finger down the vertical axis of the building. Notice that the bottom left side of the building has the same visual weight as the top right side. This gives the building asymmetrical balance.

 Hotel Nice, Nice, France.

Look at the building in image C. Imagine the building without the decorative pendulum. Does the building have symmetrical balance or asymmetrical balance? Does the pendulum make the building more interesting or less interesting? Why do you think so?

## Think Critically

1. **Focus Skill** *READING SKILL* Summarize what you learned about image B. Paraphrase the information about it on page 163. **SUMMARIZE AND PARAPHRASE**

2. How did the architect of the building in image A show unity?

3. **WRITE** Choose one of the buildings in this lesson. Imagine you are inside the building, on the top floor looking out. Write a description of what you might see.

# Design a Building

MATERIALS

- books or magazines
- pencil
- sketchbook
- white paper
- colored pencils or markers

 **PLAN**

Look at some photographs of buildings in books or magazines. Decide what kind of building you would like to design. Choose symmetrical balance or asymmetrical balance for your design. Make some sketches of your building.

**CREATE**

1. Choose your best sketch, and copy it onto white paper.

2. Use color and shape to balance the visual weight in your drawing. Use line and value to show visual texture.

3. Finish your design by drawing a setting for your building.

**REFLECT**

What kind of building did you design? What kind of setting did you place it in? What kind of balance did you show?

**Quick Tip**

Use a ruler and a round plastic lid to help you draw the geometric shapes in your design.

# I.M. Pei

*How do architects use art concepts in their designs?*

The architect I. M. Pei (PAY) has been designing buildings in the United States and around the world for more than fifty years. Born in China in 1917, Pei moved to the United States when he was seventeen to study architecture. He became well known for his use of geometric shapes and forms in large buildings made of concrete and glass. His style includes open, airy spaces for both work and entertainment.

▶ **A** I. M. Pei, architect.

▼ **B** I. M. Pei, The Rock and Roll Museum and Hall of Fame, Cleveland, Ohio.

Throughout his career, Pei has had a deep interest in the arts and education. Many of Pei's buildings are connected with art and music. These buildings include world-famous libraries, museums, and concert halls.

Look at images **B** and **C**. What geometric shapes and forms do you see? What types of balance can you see in Pei's designs?

 **I. M. Pei, Morton H. Meyerson Symphony Center,** Dallas, Texas.

# Think About Art

Imagine that you could walk through one of the buildings in image **B** or **C**. What do you think the building would look like from the inside?

 **Multimedia Biographies** Visit *The Learning Site* www.harcourtschool.com

**Vocabulary**

mural

trompe l'oeil

# Outdoor Murals

A **mural** is a painting created on a wall or ceiling. Murals can be painted on surfaces that are indoors or outdoors. Many murals are painted on the outside of buildings. Outdoor murals may give a message or tell something about a community.

Look at the mural in image **A**. It is made up of several smaller paintings by different artists. Each artist created his or her own version of a sunflower. How does this mural have unity?

 **A** **Unknown artist,** *Sunflower Mural on Fence,* Cape Town, South Africa.

**Meg Fish Saligman,**
*Common Threads,*
1998, mural paint over
sealant and primer,
8 stories tall. Philadelphia,
Pennsylvania.

## Movement

Describe what you see in image **B**. What do you think this
mural represents? The artist arranged parts of this mural to
create movement. Your eyes are guided along the triangular
shape formed by the figures. Then your eyes are guided
around the circle at the bottom of the mural.

**LOCATE IT**

The mural in image **C** is located in Los Gatos, California.

CALIFORNIA

Los Gatos

**See Maps of Museums and Art Sites, pages 206–209.**

# Trompe L'oeil

Look at the mural in image **C**. It makes you think you could walk right into the building. This mural is an example of **trompe l'oeil** (TRAWMP LOY), which means "trick the eye" in French. Trompe l'oeil is a style of painting that creates the illusion, or false idea, of a realistic three-dimensional object or scene.

Notice that the artist of image **C** used value to create movement. The darkest values draw your eye to the left side of the scene and create the illusion of depth.

**John Pugh,**
*Seven Point One,*
*(Siete Punto Uno)*
1990, acrylic on panel mounted on wall,
16 ft. × 24 ft. Los Gatos, California.

# Think Critically

1. **READING SKILL** Paraphrase the definition of *trompe l'oeil.* **SUMMARIZE AND PARAPHRASE**

2. How are the murals in this lesson alike? How are they different from each other?

3. **WRITE** Write a paragraph describing a mural you could create to tell something about your community.

# Artist's Workshop

## Create a Class Mural

**MATERIALS**

- pencil
- sketchbook
- butcher paper
- tempera paint
- large and small paintbrushes
- water bowl

### PLAN

With your classmates, brainstorm ideas for a mural. Try to express ideas or feelings about your school or community. As a group, decide which part of the mural each of you will create.

### CREATE

1. Sketch your section of the mural on a large sheet of butcher paper.

2. Work with your classmates to decide on the colors to paint your mural. Use large brushes to paint the background and large areas. Use small brushes to paint details and small areas.

### REFLECT

What ideas or feelings did you and your classmates express in your mural?

Work with your classmates as you paint to be sure that all the parts of the mural fit together well.

# Unit 5 Review and Reflect

## Vocabulary and Concepts

**Choose the letter of the word or phrase that best completes each sentence.**

1 The area around, between, and within objects is called ___.

   **A** horizon line     **C** depth

   **B** foreground     **D** space

2 The ___ is the place where the sky seems to meet the land.

   **F** horizon line     **H** space

   **G** foreground     **J** mural

3 An artwork has ___ when its parts fit together well.

   **A** depth     **C** unity

   **B** middle ground     **D** space

4 ___ means "trick the eye."

   **F** Trompe l'oeil     **H** Mural

   **G** Architecture     **J** Space

5 An artwork painted on a wall or ceiling is called a ___.

   **A** horizon line     **C** mural

   **B** vanishing point     **D** space

## Focus Skill READING SKILL

### Summarize and Paraphrase

**Reread page 148 and summarize the information in two sentences. Then paraphrase the text by retelling it in your own words. Use this chart to organize your ideas.**

| Summary: Main Ideas Only |
| --- |
| |

| Paraphrase: Main Ideas and Details in Your Own Words |
| --- |
| |

## Write About Art

**Write a summary and a paraphrase of the information on page 156. Use the chart to plan your writing.**

### REMEMBER — YOU SHOULD

- tell only the most important ideas in your summary.

- write your paraphrase as though the reader has not seen your artwork.

## Critic's Corner

**Look at *Night Scene in the Saruwaka Street in Edo* by Ando Hiroshige (hee•roh•shee•gay) to answer the questions below.**

**DESCRIBE** What is the subject of the artwork? How would you describe it?

**ANALYZE** How did the artist create a sense of distance in the artwork? What kind of perspective techniques did he use?

**INTERPRET** What feeling do you think the artist was trying to express in the artwork?

**EVALUATE** What is your opinion of this artwork compared to other artworks that show perspective techniques?

**Ando Hiroshige, *Night Scene in the Saruwaka Street in Edo,*** 1856, wood block print, colored pigments on paper, $13\frac{1}{4}$ in. × $8\frac{5}{8}$ in. Burstein Collection.

**Salvador Dalí,** *Rhinoceros Dressed in Lace,*
1955, bronze sculpture, $78\frac{7}{10}$ in. high.

## LOCATE IT

More than 1,400 works by the artist can be found in
the Salvador Dalí Museum in St. Petersburg, Florida.

**See Maps of Museums and Art Sites, pages 206–209.**

FLORIDA

St. Petersburg

# Stretch Your Imagination

## Step into the Art

Imagine that you could stand next to this sculpture. What part of it would you look at first? What do you think its textures would feel like? If you could display this sculpture anywhere, where would you place it?

## Unit Vocabulary

Abstract Expressionism

action painting

Surrealism

variety

construction

found objects

Pop Art

silkscreen

computer-generated art

**ABOUT THE ARTIST**

See Gallery of Artists, pages 240–253.

 **GO ONLINE**

Multimedia Art Glossary
Visit *The Learning Site*
www.harcourtschool.com

# Author's Purpose

**Authors have *purposes,* or reasons, for writing.
An author's purpose may be one of the following:**

- to express, or to share ideas

- to entertain, or to amuse

- to inform, or to give information

- to influence, or to make someone want to do something

**When creating an artwork, an artist has a purpose as well.**

Look at the image below, and read its title. In this image the artist has shown a person's reflection in an aquarium that seems to be under water. The artist's purpose may have been to **entertain** and to surprise the viewer by showing an object and a place that do not go together in real life.

**Ricardo Maffei,**
***Aquarium (Acuario),***
**1997, pastel on paper.
Private collection.**

Now read the passage below. Think about the author's purpose for writing it. Was it to express, to entertain, to inform, or to influence?

In the early part of the twentieth century, painters like Salvador Dalí and René Magritte began creating artworks using images from their imaginations. Their artworks often showed people and objects in realistic detail surrounded by dreamlike landscapes or backgrounds. The images were so strange and realistic at the same time that many people found the art surprising and even shocking. This was exactly what the artists had intended.

List the details that helped you figure out the author's purpose. Use a chart like this to help you.

| Author's Purpose | | |
| --- | --- | --- |
| | | |
| Detail | Detail | Detail |
| Dalí and Magritte painted images from their imaginations. | | |

# On Your Own

As you look at the artworks in this unit, use charts like the one above to help you figure out the purposes of the text and the artworks. Look back at your charts when you see questions with (Focus Skill) *READING SKILL*.

# Abstract Expressionism

**Abstract Expressionism** was an art movement that was popular in the United States in the 1950s. Abstract Expressionists wanted to express their feelings and emotions. They did not feel the need to show real objects in their artworks.

## Action Painting

Jackson Pollock, the artist of the painting in image **A**, was the best-known Abstract Expressionist. He was known for his technique of dripping, pouring, and splattering paint onto large canvases. This method of painting is called **action painting**. How would you describe this painting? What kinds of emotion does it express?

**A** Jackson Pollock, *Convergence,* 1952, oil on canvas, 93½ in. × 155 in. Albright-Knox Art Gallery, Buffalo, New York.

 **Helen Frankenthaler,** *The Bay,*
1963, acrylic on canvas, 6 ft. 8¾ in. × 6 ft. 8¾ in.
Detroit Institute of Arts, Detroit, Michigan.

The painting in image **B** is another example of Abstract Expressionism. The artist used thinned oil paints to stain, or soak, the canvas. This style was very different from the thick buildup of paint in action paintings.

**LOCATE IT**

The painting in image **A** is located in Buffalo, New York.

**179**

 **Lee Krasner,** *Bird Talk,* 1955, oil, paper, and canvas on cotton duck cloth, 58 in. × 56 in.

The Abstract Expressionist artwork in image **C** is a collage. How has the artist created unity? Now look at image **D**. What gives it unity?

 **Eric, age 9, Untitled.**

## Think Critically

1. (Focus Skill) *READING SKILL* What do you think the artist's purpose was for creating the collage in image **C**? **AUTHOR'S/ARTIST'S PURPOSE**

2. How are the paintings in images **A** and **D** alike? How are they different?

3. **WRITE** Choose an artwork from this lesson, and write a paragraph to explain your opinion of it. Be sure to support your opinion with reasons and details.

# Artist's Workshop

## Create an Action Painting

**MATERIALS**

- newsprint
- white paper
- tempera paint
- paintbrushes
- water bowl

**PLAN**

Think of the colors you would like to use in an action painting.

**CREATE**

1. Cover your work area with newsprint, and center your paper on it.

2. Using one color of paint at a time, hold your paintbrush over your paper, and drip or splatter paint onto it.

3. Drip one color over another. Try to drip paint to the edges of your paper.

4. Stand back from your painting now and then to see where you would like to add paint or change colors. Try to give your painting a sense of unity.

**REFLECT**

How did you create unity in your painting? What kind of feeling do you think it expresses?

**Quick Tip**

Drizzle the paint in layers, making it thick in some places to add texture.

# Surrealism

**Surrealism** is an art style that focuses on impossible, dreamlike images. Often, realistic objects are shown in settings where they do not belong.

What object and setting do you see in image **A**? The artist painted the object and setting in a realistic style. Notice how the light from the window shines on the left side of the apple while a shadow forms on the right side. How did the artist use values to show this? Where did the artist use linear perspective in this painting?

 René Magritte, *The Listening Room (La Chambre d'Ecoute)*, 1953, oil on canvas, 31 in. × 39$\frac{3}{8}$ in. William M. Copley Collection.

Now look at the painting in image **B**. Which part of this
painting shows an object you recognize, and which part
does not? Point out the different lines, shapes, colors, and
values you see. The artist used many different art elements
to create **variety**. Variety can make an artwork more
interesting.

Salvador Dalí,
***Telephone-Homard,***
1936, assemblage: telephone
with synthetic lobster,
$11\frac{3}{4}$ in. × $5\frac{7}{8}$ in. × $6\frac{5}{8}$ in.
Private collection.

Image **C** shows a Surrealistic sculpture. The artist combined two ordinary objects—a telephone and a lobster—in an unusual way. How did the artist use emphasis? What kind of feeling do you get from image **C**?

## Think Critically

1. **READING SKILL** What do you think the artist's purpose was for creating the artwork in image **C**? **AUTHOR'S/ARTIST'S PURPOSE**

2. How could you change image **A** from a Surrealistic scene to a realistic scene?

3. **WRITE** Write a short story about the memory that is shown in image **B**.

# Artist's Workshop

## Create a Surrealist Painting

### MATERIALS

- pencil
- sketchbook
- white paper
- tempera paint
- paintbrushes
- water bowl

**PLAN**

Think of a familiar setting. Then think of an object that does not belong in that setting. Make some sketches of the object in the setting.

**CREATE**

1. Copy your best sketch onto white paper.

2. Experiment with changing the sizes and shapes of the objects in your scene. Think of ways to add variety.

3. Paint your scene. Use tints and shades to show areas of light and shadow in the object or setting.

**REFLECT**

How does your painting show a Surrealistic scene? How did you add variety?

**Quick Tip**

Look through magazines to get ideas for settings and objects to use to create your scene.

# Maya Lin

## In what ways can an artist use unusual materials to create new art experiences?

Architect Maya Lin is best known for her designs of memorials, public parks, homes, and libraries. However, she is also a sculptor. Lin's sculptures are usually large artworks made of unusual materials. Image **A** shows a sculpture made entirely from tiny pieces of recycled glass that seems to flow out of the corner and onto the floor. A slight tremble can cause an unexpected shower of glass to flow down.

**Maya Lin,** *Avalanche,* **1998, crushed recycled glass, approximately 10 ft. x 19 ft. x 21 ft., Private collection, and in foreground,** *Untitled (Topographic Landscape),* **1997, vertical slices of trimmed particle board, 16 ft. x 18 ft. x 2 ft. Columbus Museum of Art, Columbus, Ohio.**

Image B shows one of Lin's larger sculptures. Fifty grass waves are arranged in eight rows. Each of the waves was sculpted out of soil and sand and then covered with grass. The result is a large open space for people to sit on or walk through. How would you describe the texture shown in image B?

# Think About Art

Why do you think the glass sculpture in image A is titled *Avalanche*?

 **GO ONLINE**

**Multimedia Biographies**
Visit *The Learning Site*
www.harcourtschool.com

B ▽ **Maya Lin, *The Wave Field,***
1995, earth and grass, 90 ft. x 90 ft. with waves about 5–6 ft. high. University of Michigan, Ann Arbor, Michigan.

**I**n 1981, while she was still a college student, Maya Lin entered a contest for the best design of a Vietnam War memorial. Maya Lin won the contest, and the memorial she designed was built in Washington, D.C., in 1982. The Vietnam Veterans Memorial has since become one of the city's most-visited monuments.

**Vietnam Veterans Memorial**

187

# Constructions

The artwork in image **A** is an example of a construction. A **construction** is a type of sculpture that is made by joining different pieces. It can be made from a variety of materials or from one kind of material. The construction in image **A** was made from one kind of material—wood. The artist stacked wooden boxes together to form a wall. She arranged other wooden objects, such as chair legs and railings, inside the boxes. Where do you see variety in image **A**? How did this artist create unity?

**Louise Nevelson, *Luminous Zag: Night,***
1971, painted boxes, 120 in. × 193 in. × 10¾ in.
Solomon R. Guggenheim Museum, New York, New York.

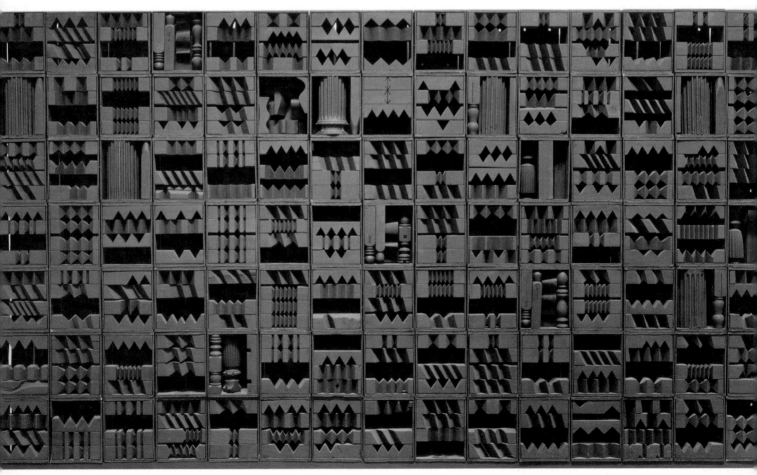

**LOCATE IT**

The artwork in image **A** is located at the Guggenheim Museum in New York City.

NEW YORK

New York City

See Maps of Museums and Art Sites, pages 206–209.

**B** Nam June Paik, *Piano Piece,* 1993, closed-circuit video sculpture, 120 in. × 84 in. × 48 in. Albright-Knox Art Gallery, Buffalo, New York.

## Assemblages and Found Objects

An assemblage is a type of construction that is made up of a variety of materials. Sometimes assemblage artists use found objects in their artworks. **Found objects** are things that an artist has found, rather than created. They include common items that have specific purposes. It is usually easy to identify found objects in an assemblage because the artist has not changed them.

Look at image **B**. What found objects did the artist use in this artwork? He created unity by using materials associated with entertainment. How did he add variety?

**189**

**Joseph Cornell,**
***Celestial Navigation,***
about 1950–1959, mixed
media shadowbox,
$9\frac{5}{8}$ in. × $16\frac{1}{4}$ in. × 4 in.
Whitney Museum of
American Art, New York,
New York.

Look at image **C**. What found objects do you see in this assemblage? How did the artist add variety? How did he use color and shape to give this artwork unity?

# Think Critically

1. **Focus Skill** *READING SKILL* What do you think the artist's purpose was for creating the artwork in image **A**? **AUTHOR'S/ARTIST'S PURPOSE**

2. How do the artworks in images **A** and **B** show rhythm?

3. **WRITE** Write two paragraphs telling how the artworks in images **A** and **C** are alike and how they are different.

# Artist's Workshop

## Create a Construction with Found Objects

**MATERIALS**

- found objects, such as yarn, paper clips, and rubber bands
- shoe box lid
- glue
- tempera paint
- paintbrushes
- water bowl

### PLAN

Gather some found objects to put together in a construction. Think of ways to add variety to your artwork.

### CREATE

1. Use the shoe box lid as the base for your construction.

2. Experiment with different arrangements of your found objects on your base.

3. Glue the objects to the base in the arrangement you like best.

4. Paint some or all of the objects in your construction. You may also paint the base.

### REFLECT

How would you describe your construction? How did you add variety?

**Quick Tip**

You may want to add variety by painting part of your construction a different color from the rest of it.

# Pop Art

**Pop Art** was an art movement that was inspired by popular media such as comic books and advertisements. Ordinary objects are the subjects of Pop Art.

## Silkscreen Prints

Andy Warhol was the best-known Pop Artist. Warhol created silkscreen prints that showed everyday items and famous people. **Silkscreen** is a process of printing. A design is created on a piece of silk and ink is forced through the silk onto paper, cloth, or another surface. For the print in image , Warhol repeated the silkscreen process, using different colors. How does the print show both unity and variety?

**Andy Warhol,**
***Six Self-Portraits,***
**1967, screen print: acrylic paint and silkscreen ink on canvas, six canvases each 22 in. × 22 in. Private collection.**

**Roy Lichtenstein,**
***Cubist Still-Life with Apple,***
about 1974, oil and magna on canvas,
20 in. × 24 in. Private collection.

Roy Lichtenstein was another famous Pop Artist. His painting style imitated what he saw in newspapers and comic books. He enlarged the tiny dots that made up the comic-strip images. He also used bold, black lines and primary colors. Look at image **B**. How did the artist add variety to the artwork? What kinds of patterns do you see?

**Social Studies Link**

Action-adventure comic strips and comic books first appeared in the United States in the 1930s. They introduced characters such as Tarzan, Dick Tracy, and Superman to young readers.

Now describe the artwork in image C. How does this artwork fit the definition of Pop Art? Point out repeated lines, shapes, and colors. How did this artist add variety to the painting? How are the artworks in images A and C alike, and how are they different?

**Wayne Thiebaud,**
***Bakery Counter,***
1962, oil on canvas,
$54\frac{7}{8}$ in. × $71\frac{7}{8}$ in.
Private collection.

## Think Critically

1. **READING SKILL** What do you think the artist's purpose was for creating the painting in image C? **AUTHOR'S/ARTIST'S PURPOSE**

2. How does image B show a Cubist art style?

3. **WRITE** Write a paragraph describing Pop Art in your own words.

# Artist's Workshop

## Create a Pop Art Collage

**MATERIALS**

- magazines
- scissors
- glue
- construction paper

**PLAN**

Find magazine photographs that represent a topic that interests you, such as sports, music, or fashion. Think about how you will arrange the photographs in a collage.

**CREATE**

1. Cut your photographs into various sizes and shapes.

2. Try several arrangements of your photographs. You might overlap them or place them side by side. Think of a way to add variety to your collage.

3. After you have chosen an arrangement, glue your photographs to a sheet of construction paper.

**REFLECT**

How does your collage show your interests? How did you add variety to your collage?

**Quick Tip**

You may want to include your own photographs or drawings in your collage.

# Vehicle Design

**A** Concept car design

**B** Computer - generated drawing

*How do designers use computers to create the cars of the future?*

Automobile companies conduct tests to find out car buyers' likes and dislikes. Vehicle designers use this information to create their designs.

Vehicle designers begin their work four to five years before the company expects to sell the car. Image **A** shows a sketch of a concept car, a design that shows many new ideas. Some designers design the outside of the car. Other designers, called color engineers, plan the car's color schemes.

Designers' sketches are scanned into a computer. Then the designers can add colors, values, textures, and even background to complete their designs. Look at image **B**. Where do you see different values? What kinds of texture do you see?

C Concept car at the
World Auto Fair

Finally, designers called clay
modelers use the computer image to
create three-dimensional models of
the concept car. These designers sculpt
a small model and then a full-size
model like the model in image C.
Both models are covered with colored
plastic to make them look realistic.

## DID YOU KNOW?

At the 2003 Detroit Auto Show in Detroit,
Michigan, Ed Welburn, a designer at
General Motors for over 30 years,
accepted an Environmental Concept
award for his work on a concept car that
is friendly to the environment.
Competitions for auto designers are held
every year, and offer chances for
designers to show their
creativity and skill.

Ed Welburn,
Executive Director
of Design, General
Motors Design
Center

## Think About Art

Name five elements of art and
principles of design that you think
would be important when designing
a car. Tell why.

# Computer Art

Computer software can do many of the things that pencils, paints, and markers can do. Art that is created on a computer is called **computer-generated art**.

Look at the computer-generated art shown in image **A**. What kinds of lines and shapes do you see? Point out the colors and textures. How did this artist add variety to the artwork?

**Angelo di Cicco,**
*No. 49D,*
2001, digital art,
2126 × 2690 pixels.
Museum of
Computer Art.

**Math Link**

The world's first general-use computer was built by two American engineers in 1946. It was 18 feet tall and 80 feet long and weighed more than 30 tons.

Joan Myerson Shrager, *Plaid Construct Swirl,* 2003, digital art. Museum of Computer Art.

Suppose you didn't know that the artwork in image B was created using a computer. What kind of materials would you think the artwork was made from?

Computer-generated art can look like a painting or even a sculpture. What kinds of shapes and colors do you see in image B? Where do you see shades and tints?

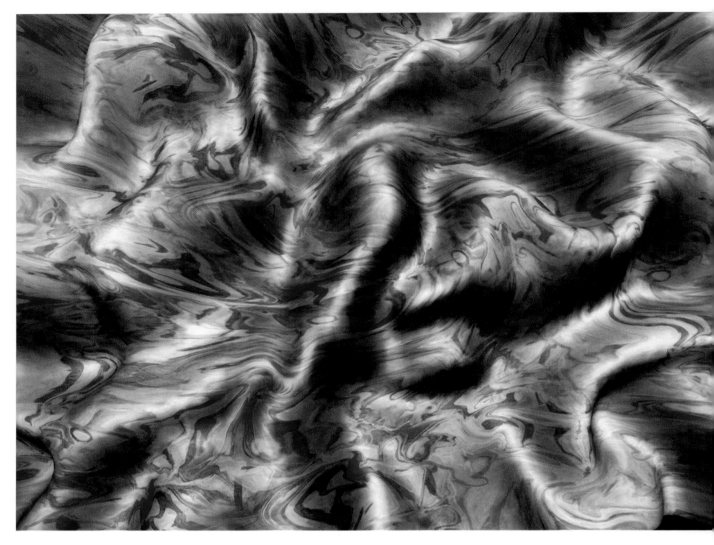

 **John Clive,**
***Annnciation II,***
2001, digital abstraction,
giclée print on paper,
$14\frac{7}{10}$ in. × 11 in. Museum
of Computer Art.

Now look at image **C**. Notice that this artist used value to create visual texture. What does this artwork remind you of? How are images **B** and **C** alike, and how are they different?

## Think Critically

1.  **READING SKILL** What do you think the artist's purpose was for creating the artwork in image **A**? **AUTHOR'S/ARTIST'S PURPOSE**

2. Compare and contrast images **A** and **B**.

3. **WRITE** Describe how you could re-create image **B** as a collage. Write what you would do first, next, and last.

# Artist's Workshop

## Create a Computer-Generated Artwork

### PLAN

Brainstorm some ideas for a design you can create on a computer. Sketch your ideas. Use simple lines and shapes.

### CREATE

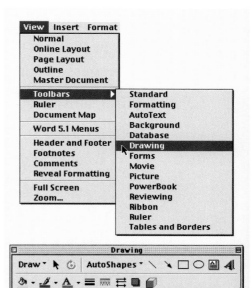

1. Choose one sketch to use as a guide.

2. Use the computer menu and drawing tools to make the simple lines and shapes from your sketch. Arrange the lines and shapes on the screen to match your sketch.

3. Add color to complete your design.

### REFLECT

How is your computer-generated artwork similar to and different from your sketch?

**Quick Tip**

You can use the drawing tools to create geometric and organic shapes.

# Unit 6 Review and Reflect

## Vocabulary and Concepts

**Choose the letter of the word or phrase that best completes each sentence.**

**1** The main characteristic of ___ was the belief in freedom to express feelings and emotions.

   **A** Cubism       **C** Surrealism

   **B** Abstract      **D** Pop Art
      Expressionism

**2** ___ focuses on dreamlike images.

   **F** Variety       **H** Surrealism

   **G** Action painting    **J** Pop Art

**3** ___ may be made up of found objects.

   **A** Assemblages     **C** Paintings

   **B** Silkscreens      **D** Variety

**4** ___ is a printing process.

   **F** Action painting    **H** Silkscreen

   **G** Construction     **J** Surrealism

**5** Using different elements in an artwork creates ___.

   **A** assemblage      **C** variety

   **B** construction     **D** Surrealism

## Focus Skill READING SKILL

### Author's Purpose

**Select an artwork from an earlier unit, and read the text about it. Think about why the artist created the piece. Use a chart to list details that help you identify the purpose.**

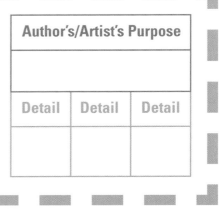

| Author's/Artist's Purpose | | |
|---|---|---|
| | | |
| Detail | Detail | Detail |
| | | |

## Write About Art

Choose a piece of your own artwork from this unit. Write a paragraph describing your purpose for creating it. Use a chart to list the details in your artwork.

### REMEMBER — YOU SHOULD

- include details to help viewers understand your purpose.

- use correct grammar, spelling, and punctuation.

## Critic's Corner

Look at *Accent in Pink* by Wassily Kandinsky to answer the questions below.

**DESCRIBE** How would you describe this artwork?

**ANALYZE** How did the artist show unity? How did he add variety?

**INTERPRET** What do you think the title of this artwork means?

**EVALUATE** What is your opinion of the way the artist used elements of art in this artwork?

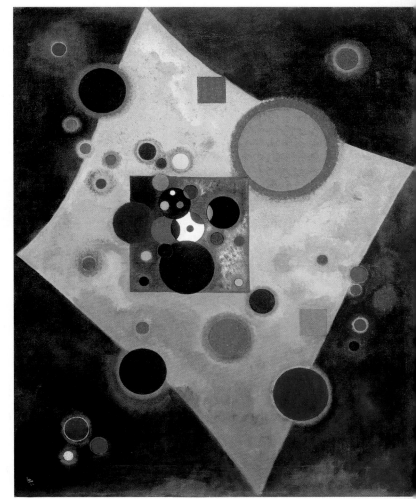

**Wassily Kandinsky,** *Accent in Pink,*
1926, oil on canvas, 101 cm × 81 cm.
National Museum of Modern Art, Paris, France.

# Student Handbook

# CONTENTS

# 15 Museums and Art Sites
## United States

CANADA

WA

MT

ND

MN

WI

OR

ID

Rapid City, South Dakota ⑧

SD

IA

CA

14

WY

NE

Los Gatos, California ⑨

NV

Great Salt Lake, Utah

UT

CO

KS

MO

AK

AZ

NM

OK

AR

Dallas, Texas

① ⑦

Fort Worth, Texas

LA

TX

San Antonio, Texas ⑥

HI

MEXICO

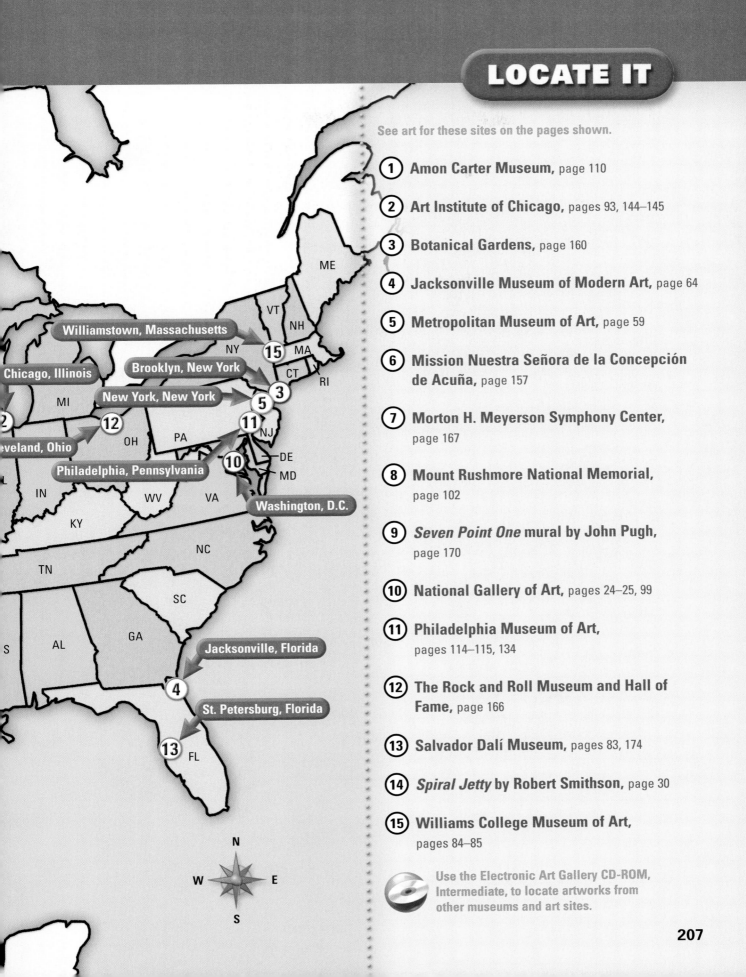

# LOCATE IT

See art for these sites on the pages shown.

1. **Amon Carter Museum,** page 110

2. **Art Institute of Chicago,** pages 93, 144–145

3. **Botanical Gardens,** page 160

4. **Jacksonville Museum of Modern Art,** page 64

5. **Metropolitan Museum of Art,** page 59

6. **Mission Nuestra Señora de la Concepción de Acuña,** page 157

7. **Morton H. Meyerson Symphony Center,** page 167

8. **Mount Rushmore National Memorial,** page 102

9. *Seven Point One* **mural by John Pugh,** page 170

10. **National Gallery of Art,** pages 24–25, 99

11. **Philadelphia Museum of Art,** pages 114–115, 134

12. **The Rock and Roll Museum and Hall of Fame,** page 166

13. **Salvador Dalí Museum,** pages 83, 174

14. *Spiral Jetty* **by Robert Smithson,** page 30

15. **Williams College Museum of Art,** pages 84–85

Use the Electronic Art Gallery CD-ROM, Intermediate, to locate artworks from other museums and art sites.

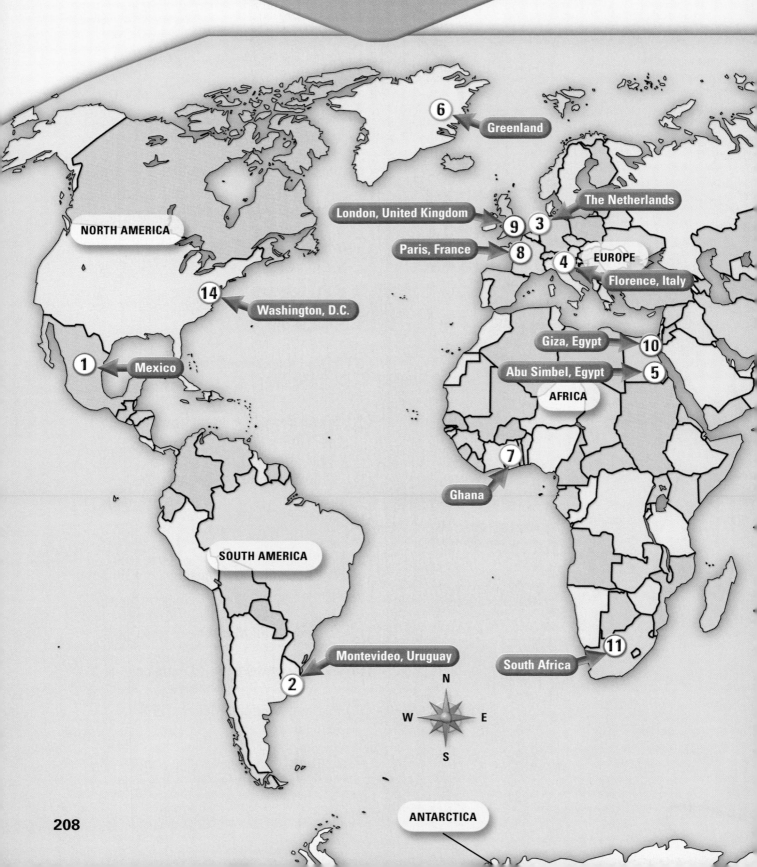

6 Greenland

NORTH AMERICA

London, United Kingdom 9 3 The Netherlands

Paris, France 8

4 EUROPE

Florence, Italy

14

Washington, D.C.

1 Mexico

Giza, Egypt 10

Abu Simbel, Egypt 5

AFRICA

7

Ghana

SOUTH AMERICA

11

South Africa

Montevideo, Uruguay

2

N

W E

S

ANTARCTICA

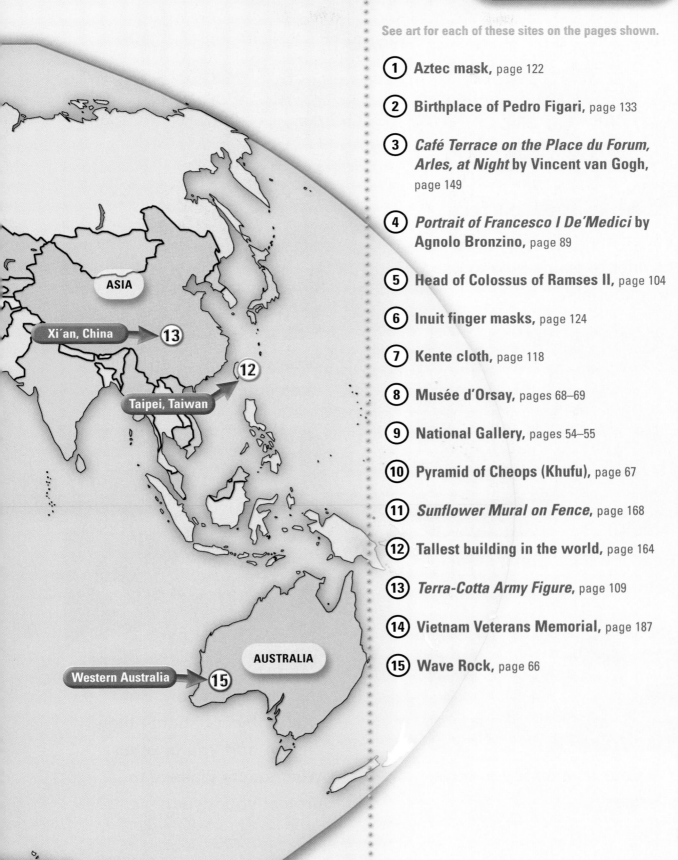

# LOCATE IT

See art for each of these sites on the pages shown.

ASIA

Xi´an, China **(13)**

Taipei, Taiwan **(12)**

AUSTRALIA

Western Australia **(15)**

# Art Safety

Listen carefully when your teacher explains how to use art materials.

Read the labels on materials before you use them.

Tell your teacher if you have allergies.

Wear a smock or apron to keep your clothes clean.

Use tools carefully. Hold sharp objects so that they cannot hurt you or others. Wear safety glasses to protect your eyes.

Use the kind of markers and inks that will not stain your clothes.

Clean up spills right away so no one will slip and fall.

Always wash your hands after using art materials.

Show respect for other students. Walk carefully around their work. Never touch classmates' work without asking first.

Cover your skin if you have a cut or scratch.

# Art Techniques

## Trying Ways to Draw

*There are lots of ways to draw. You can sketch quickly to show a rough idea of your subject, or you can draw carefully to show just how it looks to you. Try to draw every day. Keep your drawings in your sketchbook so you can see how your drawing skills improve.*

Here are some ideas for drawing. To start, get out some pencils and either your sketchbook or a sheet of paper.

### GESTURE DRAWING

Gesture drawings are quick sketches that are made with loose arm movements. The gesture drawing on the left shows a rough idea of what a baseball player looks like. The more careful drawing on the right shows details of the player's uniform and face. ▶

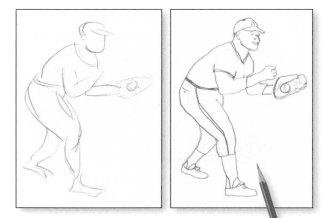

◀ **Find some photographs of people or animals.** Make gesture drawings of them. Draw quickly. Don't try to show details.

◀ **Ask a friend to pose for a gesture drawing.** Take no more than two or three minutes to finish your sketch.

## CONTOUR DRAWING

Contour drawings show only the outlines of the shapes that make up objects. They do not show the objects' color or shading. The lines that go around shapes are called **contour lines.** Use your finger to trace around the contour lines of the truck in this picture. Trace the lines around each of the shapes that make up the truck.

◀ **A blind contour drawing is made without looking at your paper as you draw.** Choose a simple object to draw, like a leaf. Pick a point on the object where you will begin drawing. Move your eyes slowly around the edge of the object. Without looking at your paper, move your pencil in the same way that your eyes move. Your first drawings may not look like the object you are looking at. Practice with different objects to improve your skill.

**Continuous contour drawings are made without** ▶ **lifting your pencil off the paper.** Draw something simple, like a chair. Look back and forth between the object and your paper. You will have to go over some lines more than once to keep from lifting your pencil off the paper.

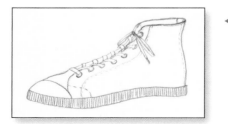

◀ **Now try making a contour drawing of another object, such as a shoe.** Look at your paper and lift your pencil whenever you want to. Then add details.

# Art Techniques

## TONAL DRAWING

**Tonal drawings show the dark and light areas of objects using tones, or shades, of one color.** They do not include contour lines. Look at the photograph at the right. Notice which areas are dark and which are light. Now look at the tonal drawing. Even without contour lines, you can tell what the drawing shows. ▶

◀ **Experiment with your pencils.** You can use **cross-hatching,** or a pattern of crossed lines, to show dark areas in a tonal drawing. Try smudging some of the lines together with your fingers. To darken large areas, use the flat edge of a dull pencil point. Use an eraser to lighten some of your marks.

**Try a tonal drawing of a simple object ▶ like a spoon.** Look at the object closely. Do not draw contour lines. Notice the shapes of the dark and light areas on the object. Use the edge of your pencil point to copy the dark shapes. Use cross-hatching in some areas. Use an eraser to lighten marks where needed.

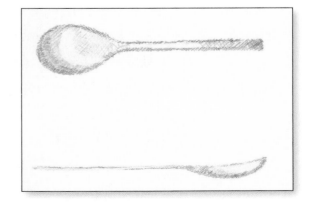

## CONTOURS AND TONES

**Try combining tonal drawing with contour drawing.** Start by making a tonal drawing of something with an interesting shape, like a backpack. Look at it carefully to see the tones of dark and light. ▶

**Then look at the object again to see its contours.** Draw contour lines around the shapes that make up the object. ▶

**You might prefer to start with a contour drawing.** Be sure you draw the outline of each shape in the object. Then add tones with shading or cross-hatching. ▼

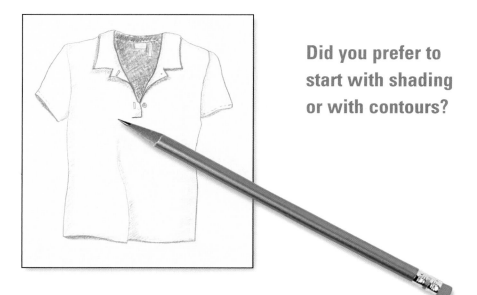

**Did you prefer to start with shading or with contours?**

215

# Art Techniques

## Experimenting with Paint

*Working with colors is always fun. Experimenting with paint will help you learn about color and how you can use it in your artwork.*

These are some things you should have when you paint: old newspapers to cover your work area, an old shirt to cover your clothes, tempera paints or watercolors, plastic plates or plastic egg cartons for mixing paint, paper, paintbrushes, a jar or bowl of water, and paper towels.

### TEMPERA PAINTS

**Tempera paints** are water-based, so they are easy to clean up. The colors are bright and easy to mix.

### GETTING STARTED

**Start experimenting with different kinds of brushstrokes.** Try painting with lots of paint on the brush and then with the brush almost dry. (You can dry the paintbrush by wiping it across a paper towel.) Make a brushstroke by twisting the paintbrush on your paper. See how many different brushstrokes you can make by rolling, pressing, or dabbing the brush on the paper.

**Now load your brush with as much paint as it will** ▶ **hold, and make a heavy brushstroke.** Use a craft stick or another tool to draw a pattern in it.

**Use what you've learned to paint a picture.** Use as many different brushstrokes as you can. ▶

216

## MIXING COLORS

Even if you have only a few colors of tempera paint, you can mix them to make almost any color you want. Use the **primary colors** red, yellow, and blue to create the **secondary colors** orange, green, and violet.

◀ **Mix dark and light colors.** To make darker colors (**shades**), add black. To make lighter colors (**tints**), add white. See how many shades and tints of a single color you can make.

## TECHNIQUES TO TRY

**Pointillism is a technique that makes the viewer's eyes mix the colors.** Use colors, such as blue and yellow, that make a third color when mixed. Make small dots of color close together without letting the dots touch. In some areas, place the two different colors very close together. Stand back from your paper. What happens to the colors as your eyes "mix" them? ▶

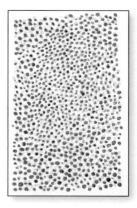

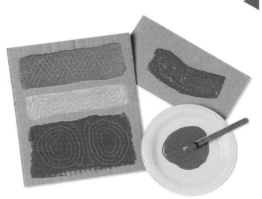

◀ **Impasto is a technique that creates a thick or bumpy surface on a painting.** You can create an impasto painting by building up layers of paint, or by thickening your paint with a material such as wheat paste. Mix some paint and wheat paste in a small bowl. Spread some of the mixture on a piece of cardboard. Experiment with tools such as a toothpick, a plastic fork, or a comb to make textures in the impasto. Mix more colors and use them to make an impasto picture or design.

# Art Techniques

## WATERCOLORS

**Watercolors** usually come in little dry cakes. You have to add the water! So keep a jar of clean water and some paper towels nearby as you paint. Use paper that is made for watercolors.

## GETTING STARTED

**Dip your paintbrush in water and then dab it on one of the watercolors.** Try a brushstroke. Watercolors are transparent. Since you can see through them, the color on your paper will never be as dark as the color of the cake. Use different amounts of water. What happens to the color when you use a lot of water?

**Now rinse your brush in water and use another color.** Try different kinds of brushstrokes—thick and thin, squiggles and waves, dots and blobs. Change colors often.

**Try using one color on top of a different color that is already dry.** Work quickly. If your brushstrokes are too slow, the dry color underneath can become dull. If you want part of your painting to be white, don't paint that part. The white comes from the color of the paper.

218

## MIXING COLORS

**Experiment with mixing watercolors right on your paper.** Try painting with a very wet brush. Add a wet color on top of, or just touching, another wet color. Try three colors together. ▶

**You can also mix colors on your paintbrush.** Dip your brush into one color and then another before you paint. Try it with green and yellow. Clean your paintbrush and try some other combinations. To clean any paint cakes that you have used for mixing, just wipe them with a paper towel. ▶

## TECHNIQUES TO TRY

◀ **Try making a watercolor wash.** Start with a patch of dark green. Then clean your paintbrush and get it very wet. Use it to "wash" the color down the page. (You can also do this with a foam brush or a sponge.)

You can wet all of one side of the paper, brush a stroke of color across it, and let the color spread. Try two or three color washes together. For a special effect, sprinkle salt onto the wet paper.

**Try using tempera paints and watercolors together.** ▶
Start with a two-color watercolor wash. Let it dry. Then use several kinds of brushstrokes to paint a design on top of the wash with tempera paint.

Remember these techniques when you paint designs or pictures. Be sure to clean your paintbrushes and work area when you have finished.

# Art Techniques

## Working with Clay

*Clay is a special kind of mud or earth that holds together and is easy to shape when it is mixed with water. Clay objects can be fired, or heated at a high temperature, to make them harden. They can also be left in the air to dry until hard.*

To make an object with clay, work on a clean, dry surface. (A brown paper bag makes a good work surface.) Have some water handy. If the clay starts to dry out, add a few drops of water at a time. When you are not working with the clay, store it in a plastic bag to keep it moist.

**You can use an assortment of tools.** Use a rolling pin to make flat slabs of clay. Use a plastic knife or fork, keys, a comb, or a pencil to add texture or designs to the objects you make out of clay.

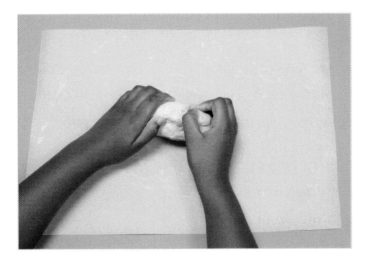

**Start working with a piece of clay by making sure it has no air bubbles in it.** Press it down, fold it over, and press it down again. This process is called **kneading**.

## MODELING

**Try making different forms with your clay.** ▶ If one of your forms reminds you of an animal or a person, continue to mold the form by pinching and pulling the clay.

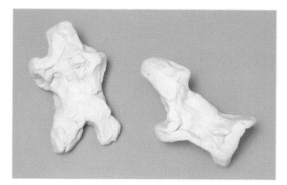

◀ **You can join two pieces of clay together.** Carve small lines on the edges that will be joined. This is called **scoring**. Then use **slip,** or clay dissolved in water, to wet the surfaces. Press the pieces together and smooth the seams.

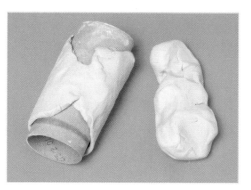

**To make a bigger form, wrap a slab of clay around a tube or crumpled newspaper.**

Try adding patterns, textures, or details to your form. Experiment with your tools. Press textured objects into the clay and lift them off. Brush a key across the clay. Press textured material like burlap into your clay, lift it off, and add designs. If you change your mind, smooth the clay with your fingers and try something else.

# Art Techniques

## USING SLABS

**Roll your clay out flat, to between $\frac{1}{4}$ inch and $\frac{1}{2}$ inch thick.** Shape the clay by molding it over something like a bowl or crumpled paper. ▶

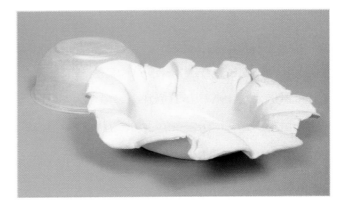

◀ **To make a slab box, roll your clay out flat.** Use a plastic knife to cut six equal-sized squares or rectangles for the bottom, top, and sides of your box. Score the edges, and then let the pieces dry until they feel like leather.

**Join the pieces together with slip.** ▶ Then smooth the seams with your fingers.

## USING COILS

**To make a coil pot, roll pieces of clay against a hard surface.** Use your whole hand to make long clay ropes. ▶

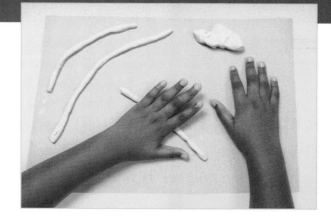

◀ **Make the bottom of your pot by coiling a clay rope into a circle.** Smooth the seams with your fingers. To build the sides, attach coils of clay on top of one another. Score and wet the pieces with slip as you attach them. Smooth the inside as you work. You may smooth the outside or let the coils show.

## MAKING A CLAY RELIEF ▶

**A relief is a sculpture raised from a surface.** To make a relief, draw a simple design on a slab of clay. Roll some very thin ropes and attach them to the lines of the design. This is called the **additive method** because you are adding clay to the slab.

◀ **You can also make a relief sculpture by carving a design out of your clay slab.** This is called the **subtractive method** because you are taking away, or subtracting, clay from the slab.

# Art Techniques

## Exploring Printmaking

*When you make a print, you transfer color from one object to another. If you have ever left a muddy footprint on a clean floor, you know what a print is. Here are some printmaking ideas to try.*

### COLLOGRAPH PRINTS

A **collograph** is a combination of a **collage** and a **print**. To make a collograph, you will need cardboard, glue, paper, newspapers, a brayer (a roller for printing), printing ink or paint, a flat tray such as a foam food tray, and some paper towels or sponges. You will also need some flat objects to include in the collage. Try things like old keys, string, lace, paper clips, buttons, small shells, or burlap.

**Arrange objects on the cardboard** ▶ **in a pleasing design.** Glue the objects to the surface, and let the glue dry.

**Prepare your ink while the collage** ▶ **is drying.** Place a small amount of ink or paint on your foam tray. Roll the brayer through the ink until it is evenly coated. Gently run the brayer over the collage. Most of the ink should be on the objects.

**Now press a piece of paper onto** ▶ **the inked collage.** Gently rub the paper. Peel off the paper and let the ink dry. You've made a collograph!

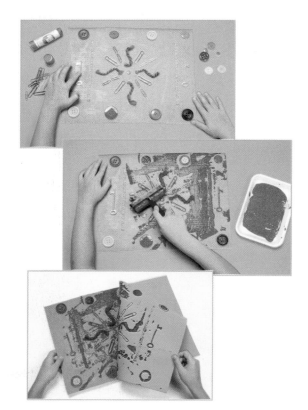

## MULTICOLOR PRINTS

You can use different colors of tempera paint to make a multicolor print with repeated shapes. You will need poster board or a foam tray (such as a food tray), cardboard, scissors, glue, paper, water, tempera paint, and a paintbrush.

**First cut out some interesting shapes from the poster board or foam tray.** Carve or poke holes and lines into the shapes. ▶

**Arrange the shapes on the cardboard to make an interesting design.** Glue down the pieces. When the glue is dry, paint the shapes with different colors of tempera paint. Try not to get paint on the cardboard. ▶

◀ **While the paint is wet, place a sheet of paper on top of your design.** Gently rub the paper, and peel it off carefully. Let the paint dry.

After the shapes dry, paint them again with different colors. Print the same paper again, but turn it so that the designs and colors overlap.

**Try using different colors, paper, and objects to make prints.**

# Art Techniques

## Displaying Your Artwork

*Displaying your artwork is a good way to share it.*
*Here are some ways to make your artwork look its best.*

### DISPLAYING ART PRINTS

Select several pictures that go together well. Line them up along a wall
or on the floor. Try grouping the pictures in different ways. Choose an
arrangement that you like. Attach a strong string across a wall. Use
clothespins or paper clips to hang your pictures on the string.

**Make a frame.** Use a piece of cardboard that is longer and
wider than the art. In the center of the cardboard, draw a rectangle
that is slightly smaller than your picture. Have an adult help you
cut out the rectangle. Then decorate your frame. Choose colors
and textures that look good with your picture. You can paint the
frame or use a stamp to print a design on it. You can add texture
by gluing strips of cardboard or rows of buttons onto your frame.

**Mount your picture.** Tape the corners of your
artwork to the back of the frame. Cut a solid piece of
cardboard the same size as the frame. Then glue the
framed artwork to the cardboard. Tape a loop of
thread on the back. Hang up your framed work.

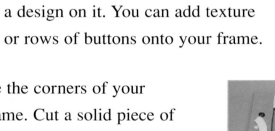

## DISPLAYING SCULPTURES

To display your clay objects or sculptures, find a location where your work will be safe from harm. Look for a display area where people won't bump into your exhibit or damage your work.

**Select several clay objects or sculptures that go together well.** Try grouping them in different ways. Place some of the smaller objects on boxes. When you find an arrangement that you like, remove your artworks, tape the boxes to the table, and drape a piece of cloth over the boxes. Pick a plain cloth that will look good under your artworks, try adding a few interesting folds in the cloth, and place your artworks back on the table.

**Now invite your friends and family over to see your work!**

# Line

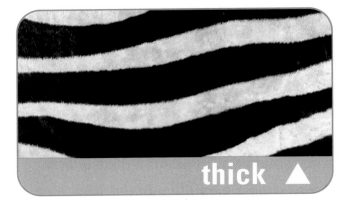

**thick** ▲

**vertical** ▶

**thin** ▲

**wavy** ▲

**straight** ▼

**horizontal** ▲

**zigzag** ▼

# Shape

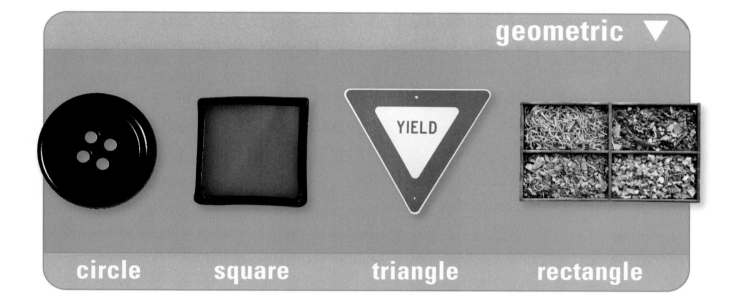

**geometric** ▼

| circle | square | triangle | rectangle |

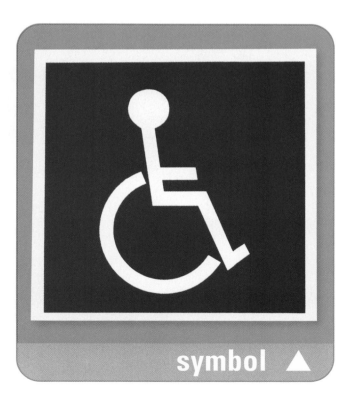

**symbol** ▲

▼ **organic**

229

# Color and Value

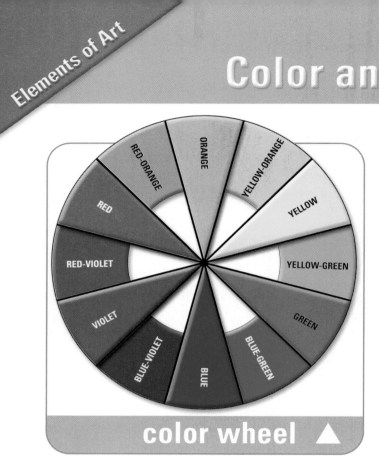

**color wheel** ▲

**cool colors** ▲

**warm colors** ▲

**complementary colors** ▲

▼ **value**

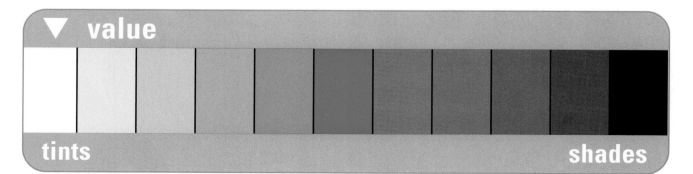

tints        shades

The color wheel labels (clockwise): ORANGE, YELLOW-ORANGE, YELLOW, YELLOW-GREEN, GREEN, BLUE-GREEN, BLUE, BLUE-VIOLET, VIOLET, RED-VIOLET, RED, RED-ORANGE

# Texture

bumpy ▲

▼ soft

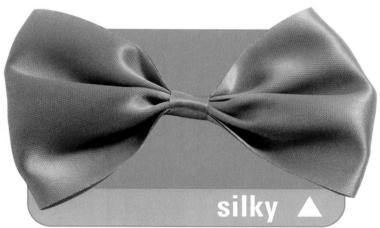

silky ▲

▼ smooth

rough ▲

# Form

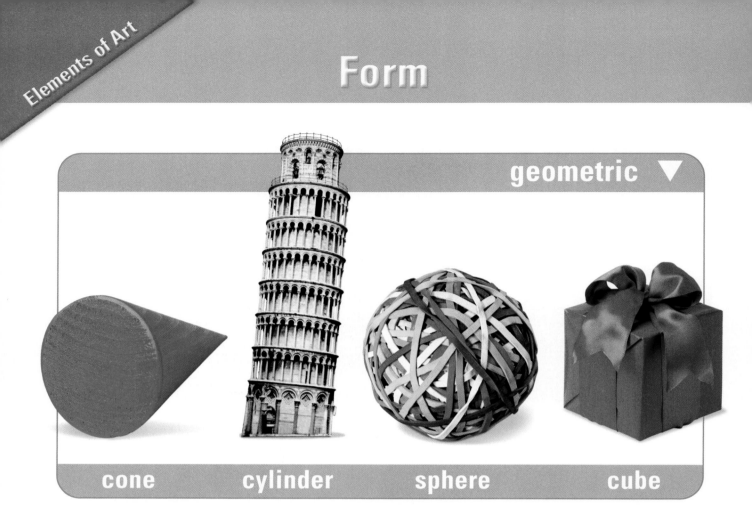

geometric ▼

| cone | cylinder | sphere | cube |

organic ▲

# Space

overlapping ▼

atmospheric perspective ▼

background ▶

middle ground ▶

foreground ▶

positive ▶

◀ negative

▲ linear perspective

# Pattern

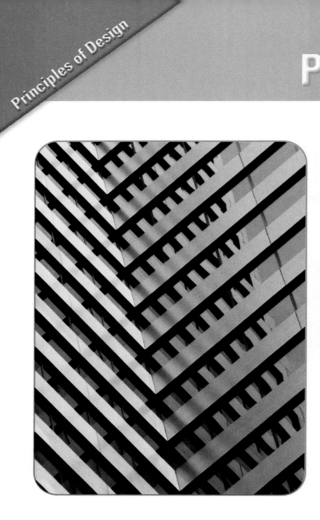

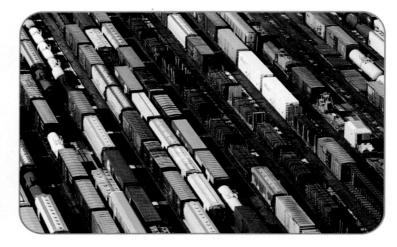

# Proportion

# Balance

▼ radial

asymmetrical ▲

symmetrical ▲

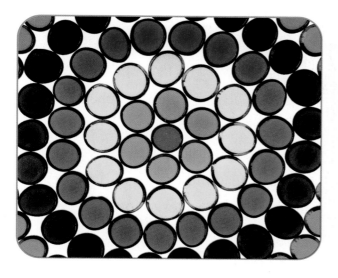

# Gallery of Artists

### Meredith Brooks Abbott

(1938– ) United States, painter. Abbott grew up in rural California with a great appreciation for the land. She paints Impressionistic landscapes. **page 58**

### Josef Albers

(1888–1976) Germany, painter. Albers studied art while teaching elementary school. He is best known for his abstract paintings of overlapping monochromatic squares. **page 60**

### Giacomo Balla

(1871–1958) Italy, painter. Balla was particularly interested in how light and movement were represented in his work. His paintings are considered very inventive. **page 100**

### Bruce Barnbaum

(1943– ) United States, photographer. Barnbaum is recognized as one of the finest photographers today. His work is featured in many art galleries in the United States. **page 72**

### Thomas Hart Benton

(1889–1975) United States, painter. Benton began his career as a cartoonist. He later became known for his pictures of rural America. **page 26**

### Albert Bierstadt

(1830–1902) United States, painter. Born in Germany, Bierstadt [BEER•stat] spent his childhood in Massachusetts. He is best known for his landscapes of the American West. **page 152**

## John Biggers

(1924–2001) United States, painter. Biggers was a former teacher who believed that art can help African Americans better understand their culture. His paintings, drawings, and murals have won many awards. **page 143**

## Gutzon Borglum

(1867–1941) United States, sculptor. Borglum was a successful painter before he became well known as a sculptor. His best-known sculptures are of the four U.S. Presidents shown on the face of Mount Rushmore. **page 102**

## Victor Brauner

(1903–1966) Romania, painter/sculptor. Brauner is known for his artworks of the human figure. He was heavily influenced by the Surrealists. **page 183**

## Agnolo Bronzino

(1503–1572) Italy, painter. Bronzino was a court artist to the Medici family. **page 89**

## Gustave Caillebotte

(1848–1894) France, painter. Caillebotte's [ky•yuh•bawt] paintings show bold perspectives and delicate light. **page 144**

## Bobbi A. Chukran

(1956– ) United States, folk artist. Chukran's inspiration comes mostly from nature. **page 50**

## Angelo di Cicco

(1953– ) Italy, digital artist/painter. Di Cicco is a physician who enjoys painting in his spare time. **page 198**

# Gallery of Artists

 **John Clive**
England, digital artist. Clive directs film, theatre, and commercials. **page 200**

 **Joseph Cornell**
(1903–1972) United States, sculptor. Cornell was an assemblage artist best known for his glass-fronted shadow boxes. **pages 80, 190**

 **Jean Baptiste Camille Corot**
(1796–1875) France, painter/printmaker. Corot believed that a sketch captured a nature scene better than a painting. **page 148**

 **Salvador Dalí**
(1904–1989) Spain, painter. Dalí [DAH•lee] was the most famous Surrealist artist. He also designed jewelry, advertisements, costumes, and stage sets. **pages 83, 174, 184**

 **Edgar Degas**
(1834–1917) France, painter. Degas [duh•GAH] was fascinated by photographic techniques. He painted many pictures of dancers, often in rehearsal or backstage. **page 98**

 **Raymond Depardon**
(1942– ) France, photographer. Depardon is self-taught. His more recent work has been in film and advertising. **page 78**

 **Robert S. Duncanson**
(about 1821–1872) United States, painter. Duncanson is best known for his landscapes. He is thought to be the first African American artist not only to make a living from selling his paintings but also to become famous for them. **page 24**

## W. Herbert Dunton

(1878–1936) United States, painter/illustrator. Dunton is considered one of America's most popular artists of cowhand and frontier life. **page 136**

## M. C. Escher

(1898–1972) Holland, graphic artist. Escher [ESH•er] studied architecture but became a graphic artist instead. He is famous for his drawings that surprise viewers with optical illusions. **page 73**

## Marisol Escobar

(1930– ) France, sculptor. Escobar creates life-size figure arrangements. Her work is heavily influenced by Mexican and American folk art. **pages 106–107**

## Lyonel Feininger

(1871–1956) United States, painter/printmaker/illustrator. Feininger's work combines qualities of both Cubism and Expressionism. **page 99**

## Pedro Figari

(1861–1938) Uruguay, painter. Figari had a degree in law but was gifted in art. His paintings celebrate Uruguayan culture. **page 133**

## Norman Foster

(1935– ) England, architect. Foster is considered one of the leading modernist architects. **page 163**

## Helen Frankenthaler

(1928– ) United States, painter/printmaker. Frankenthaler was one of the leading artists of the Abstract Expressionist movement. **page 179**

# Gallery of Artists

## Paul Gauguin

(1848–1903) France, painter. Gauguin [goh•GAN] was a sailor in the French navy and a stockbroker before he became a painter. He moved to the tropical island of Tahiti in 1895 where he lived and painted for the rest of his life. **page 48**

## William James Glackens

(1870–1938) United States, painter/illustrator. Glackens began his art career as an illustrator. He went on to study painting and later produced artworks in a very realistic style. **page 146**

## Glenna Goodacre

(1939– ) United States, sculptor.

**page 102**

## Sante Graziani

(1920– ) United States, muralist. Graziani drew medical illustrations while he served in the United States Army. He was influenced by Surrealism and by famous paintings of the past. **page 140**

## Juan Gris

(1887–1927) France, painter. Gris [GREES] was considered one of the leading Cubist painters in France, where he spent most of his life as an artist. He was a friend of the Cubist painter Pablo Picasso. **page 93**

## Jack Gunter

United States, painter. Gunter has also worked with photography and ceramics. **page 150**

## Richard Haas

(1936– ) United States, muralist/printmaker/architect. Haas has created more than 120 murals and is renowned for his trompe l'oeil paintings. **page 137**

## Ole Juul Hansen

**page 44**

## Frederick Childe Hassam

(1859–1935) United States, painter/printmaker. Hassam painted landscapes of New England and rural New York. **page 138**

## Ando Hiroshige

(1797–1858) Japan, painter/printmaker. Hiroshige [hee•roh•shee•gay] became famous for his many landscape paintings and views of the city of Edo, now called Tokyo. **page 173**

## David Hockney

(1937– ) United States, mixed media. Born in England, Hockney now lives in southern California. He was eleven years old when he decided he wanted to be an artist. Hockney has said, "The smallest event can become a story if you tell it in the right way." **page 79**

## Winslow Homer

(1836–1910) United States, painter/illustrator. Fascinated by the ocean, Winslow Homer painted many works that show the coast of Maine, where he lived. Many of his works show people struggling against powerful seas. **page 84**

## Don Jacot

(1949– ) United States, painter. Don Jacot [jahk•OH] paints in the photorealistic style. **page 154**

# Gallery of Artists

## Alexej von Jawlensky

(1864–1941) Russia, painter. Von Jawlensky [yah•VLEN•skee] spent much of his early artistic career traveling, which introduced him to a variety of artists, techniques, and theories. **pages 29, 92**

## Bernadine Jendrzejczak

United States, folk artist. Jendrzejczak (yin•JAY•chek) is known for her traditional Polish paper cuttings. **page 129**

## Frida Kahlo

(1907–1954) Mexico, painter. Kahlo is best known for her self-portraits. Many of her paintings show her Mexican heritage. **page 90**

## Wassily Kandinsky

(1866–1944) Russia, painter. Kandinsky is often considered one of the founders of abstract art. **page 203**

## Warren Kimble

United States, folk artist. Kimble's paintings focus on nature scenes near his Vermont home. **page 139**

## Paul Klee

(1879–1940) Switzerland, painter. Klee's [KLAY] paintings, drawings, and etchings have been described as childlike. Klee was a professional violinist before becoming an artist. **pages 46–47**

## Lee Krasner

(1908–1984) United States, painter. Krasner was married to artist Jackson Pollock. She created expressive paintings, abstract still-lifes, and collages. **page 180**

## Roy Lichtenstein

(1923–1997) United States, painter. Lichtenstein [LIK•tuhn•styn] was one of the best-known American painters in the Pop Art movement. His most famous paintings imitate comic strips. **page 193**

## Maya Lin

(1959– ) United States, sculptor. Maya Lin is best known for her Vietnam Veterans Memorial in Washington, D.C. Lin has also created small sculptures and stage sets. **pages 186–187**

## Carmen Lomas Garza

(1948– ) United States, illustrator. Lomas Garza is best known for her artworks that show Chicano family life. **page 130**

## Ricardo Maffei

(1953– ) Chile, painter. **page 176**

## René Magritte

(1898–1967) Belgium, painter. Magritte [ma•GREET] once worked as a wallpaper designer. Many of his paintings include patterns like those used on wallpaper. Magritte often painted dreamlike scenes. **pages 113, 182**

## Franz Marc

(1880–1916) Germany, painter. Marc used bright color to show emotion in his paintings. He co-founded the Blue Rider group, which included other artists who also used color in an expressive way. **page 32**

# Gallery of Artists

### Henri Matisse

(1869–1954) France, painter. Matisse [mah•TEES] was the leader of a group of artists who used bright colors and strong brushstrokes. This was considered so shocking that the artists were known as the Fauves [FOHVZ], or "wild beasts." **pages 76–77**

### Colleen Meechan

United States, painter. Meechan is a landscape painter whose artworks depict tropical scenes. **page 40**

### Amedeo Modigliani

(1884–1920) Italy, painter/sculptor. Modigliani [moh•deel•YAH•nee] was influenced by African art. The facial features in his paintings and sculptures often resembled those in African masks. **pages 126–127**

### Claude Monet

(1840–1926) France, painter. Monet [moh•NAY] and his fellow French Impressionist painters became known for painting with small patches of color that blend together from a distance. Though not well accepted by the art world of his time, Monet is now considered a master artist. **pages 42, 68**

### Berthe Morisot

(1841–1895) France, painter/printmaker. Morisot [moh•ree•zoh] worked in art museums, where she painted copies of original masterpieces. Her own paintings often showed family scenes. **page 69**

### Grandma Moses

(1860–1961) United States, painter. Grandma Moses began painting in her seventies. Her folk art paintings frequently show rural life. **page 132**

## Louise Nevelson

(about 1900–1988) United States, sculptor. Nevelson is well known for her large assemblages. **page 188**

## Mike O'Brien

United States, sculptor. O'Brien is the exhibits coordinator for Texas Parks and Wildlife, a department of that state. **page 104**

## Isy Ochoa

**page 63**

## Georgia O'Keeffe

(1887–1986) United States, painter. O'Keeffe grew up on a farm in Wisconsin. By the age of twelve, she knew she wanted to be an artist. Many of her most famous paintings show close-up views of flowers. **pages 34, 37**

## Nam June Paik

(1932– ) Korea, composer/video artist. Paik became known as a composer of electronic music and later began making video art and TV sculptures. **page 189**

## I. M. Pei

(1917– ) China, architect. Pei's [PAY] works include the Dallas City Hall building, part of the Louvre Museum in Paris, and the Rock and Roll Hall of Fame and Museum in Cleveland, Ohio. **pages 166–167**

## Pablo Picasso

(1881–1973) Spain, painter. Picasso was one of the greatest artists of the twentieth century. He helped found a movement in painting called Cubism. Picasso was influenced by the style of African sculpture. **pages 49, 94**

# Gallery of Artists

### Horace Pippin
(1888–1946) United States, painter. Pippin began painting seriously after his right arm was partially paralyzed as the result of an injury. Many of his works show scenes from the Bible or from the daily life of African American families. **page 53**

### Jackson Pollock
(1912–1956) United States, painter. Pollock's [PAHL•uhk] paintings express powerful moods without showing objects. He was known for a style of Abstract Expressionism called Action Painting. **page 178**

### Anna Pugh
England, folk artist. Anna Pugh's work has been influenced by middle-eastern painting styles. **page 86**

### John Pugh
United States, painter. Pugh is best known for his detailed trompe l'oeil murals, which trick the eye. **page 170**

### Man Ray
(1890–1976) United States, photographer/painter/sculptor. Man Ray was best known for the unusual subjects in his artworks. He was part of the Surrealist movement. **page 110**

### Frederic S. Remington
(1861–1909) United States, sculptor/painter. Although born in New York, Remington spent a good deal of time in the frontier of the American West, documenting the lives of soldiers and cowhands. **pages 56, 110**

## Faith Ringgold

(about 1930– ) United States, painter/sculptor. Ringgold's paintings and quilts reflect the issues facing African Americans and women. **page 114**

## Thomas Rogers

United States, sculptor. Rogers is best known for his image of an eagle, which appears on the tail side of the Sacagawea American coin. **page 102**

## Henri Rousseau

(1844–1910) France, painter. Rousseau [roo•SOH] taught himself to paint and began painting full time at age forty-nine. The ideas for his paintings came from gardens and illustrated books. **page 59**

## Meg Fish Saligman

United States, muralist. **page 169**

## Matiros Sarian

(1880–1972) Armenia, painter/museum director. Sarian painted many fantasy scenes, often based on folktales. His style is very colorful and bright, with rhythmic patterns. **page 43**

## Georges Seurat

(1859–1891) France, painter. Seurat [suh•RAH] painted huge compositions that seem to shimmer. His technique of showing light by using tiny dots of contrasting colors is called Pointillism. **pages 54, 153**

## Joan Myerson Shrager

United States, painter/sculptor/ digital artist. Shrager experiments with a variety of media and techniques in her art. **page 199**

## Paul Sierra

(1944– ) Cuba, painter. Sierra's use of bright color and vast spaces often gives his paintings a dreamlike quality. **page 38**

## Robert Smithson

(1938–1973) United States, sculptor. *Spiral Jetty*, one of Smithson's most famous works, is an example of environmental art. Also called land art or earthworks art, this kind of art involves large-scale changes to the surface of the Earth. **page 30**

## Joaquín Sorolla y Bastida

(1863–1923)

Spain, painter. Sorolla y Bastida [soh•ROH•yah ee bahs•TEE•dah] used the Mediterranean seashore as his inspiration for beach scene paintings. **page 70**

## Alice Kent Stoddard

(1885–1976) United States, painter. Stoddard is known for her portraits and landscapes. **page 88**

## Wayne Thiebaud

(1920– ) United States, painter.

Thiebaud [TEE•boh] was born in Mesa, Arizona, and held various art-related jobs in New York and California. He is best known for his texture paintings of ice cream, cakes, and hot dogs. **page 194**

## Vincent van Gogh

(1853–1890) Holland, painter. Van Gogh [van GOH] sold only one painting when he was alive, but today he is recognized as one of the most famous painters in history. He used bright colors, thick oil paint, and visible brushstrokes. **pages 33, 149**

## José María Velasco

(1840–1912) Mexico, painter. Velasco [vay•LAHS•koh] was known as a landscape painter. He is considered a "scientific" artist because he created many sketches of nature and the human body. **page 29**

## Diego Velázquez

(1599–1660) Spain, painter. Velázquez [vay•LAHS•kes] was the court painter for King Philip IV of Spain. One of the artist's favorite techniques was to focus intense light on his subjects and set them against dark backgrounds. **page 96**

## Robert Wagstaff

United States, painter. Wagstaff was born and raised in Hawaii. Native Hawaiian plants and animals are often the subjects of his artworks. **page 39**

## Andy Warhol

(about 1928–1987) United States, painter. Warhol was one of the most important artists in the Pop Art movement. He used familiar commercial images but played with their colors and sizes, often repeating the images. **page 192**

## Memphis Wood

United States, folk artist. Wood has been a member of the Jacksonville, Florida, art community for years. She has taught all over the state. **page 64**

# Glossary

*The Glossary contains important art terms and their definitions. Each word is respelled as it would be in a dictionary. When you see this mark ˈ after a syllable, pronounce that syllable with more force than the other syllables.*

| a add | e end | o odd | o͞o pool | oi oil | th this | ə = | a in above |
|-------|-------|-------|----------|--------|---------|-----|------------|
| ā ace | ē equal | ō open | u up | ou pout | zh vision | | e in sicken |
| â care | i it | ô order | û burn | ng ring | | | i in possible |
| ä palm | ī ice | o͝o took | yo͞o fuse | th thin | | | o in melon |
| | | | | | | | u in circus |

## A

**abstract art** [abˈstrakt ärt] Art that does not look realistic. Artists may show either real objects in unusual ways or no real objects at all. (page 92)

**Abstract Expressionism** [abˈstrakt ik•spreshˈən•iz•əm] A twentieth-century art movement in which artists believed in the freedom to express feelings and emotions. (page 178)

**action painting** [akˈshən pānˈting] A technique of dripping, pouring, and splattering paint onto large canvases. (page 178)

**actual line** [akˈsho͞o•əl līn] A line that clearly outlines an object. (page 29)

**actual lines**

**architect** [ärˈkə•tekt] A person who designs buildings. (page 162)

**artwork** [ärtˈwûrk] A piece of art, such as a drawing, a painting, or a sculpture. (page 28)

**assemblage** [ə•semˈblij] A sculpture made from various objects and materials. (page 80)

254

**asymmetrical balance**

[ā•sə•me′tri•kəl ba′ləns] A type of balance achieved when two sides of an artwork are different but visually equal in weight. (page 130)

**atmospheric perspective**

[at•məs•fēr′ik pər•spek′tiv] A technique used to create a sense of depth in a two-dimensional artwork by using dull colors and fuzzy edges in the background. (page 152)

**background** [bak′ground] The part of an artwork that seems farthest from the viewer. (page 148)

background

**blending** [blen′ding] Mixing or smudging areas in an artwork to create gradual value changes. (page 74)

**close-up view** [klōs•up vyōō] A detailed view of an object or part of an object. (page 34)

**collage** [kə•läzh′] An artwork made by gluing materials, such as paper or cloth, onto a flat surface. (page 50)

**color scheme** [kul′ər skēm] An artist's plan for choosing colors for an artwork. (page 40)

**complementary colors**

[kom•plə•men′tər•ē kul′ərz] Colors that are opposite each other on the color wheel. (page 39)

**complementary colors**

**computer-generated art**

[kəm•pyōō′tər•jen′ər•ā•təd ärt] Artwork that is created with software on a computer. (page 198)

**construction** [kən•struk′shən] A type of sculpture that is made of parts joined together. It can be made from a variety of materials or from one kind of material. (page 188)

**contrast** [kon′trast] A sharp difference between two things, making one or both stand out. (page 39)

**cool colors** [kool kul′ərz] The colors blue, green, and violet. These colors create a calm, peaceful mood. (page 42)

**cool colors**

**Cubism** [kyoo′biz•əm] A style of abstract art in which the artist may show more than one view of a subject at the same time. (page 93)

**depth** [depth] The appearance of space or distance in a two-dimensional artwork. (page 148)

**distortion** [dis•tôr′shən] A technique used to change the way a subject looks, by bending, stretching, or twisting its shape. (page 93)

**distortion**

**dominant color** [dom′ə•nənt kul′ər] The color a viewer sees most in an artwork. (page 58)

**emphasis** [em′fə•sis] The special importance given to one part of an artwork. (page 78)

**facial proportions** [fā′shəl prə•pôr′shənz] The way the features of the human face, such as eyes, nose, and mouth, are related to each other in size and placement. (page 89)

**fiber** [fī′bər] A material such as cloth, yarn, or thread. (page 64)

**fiber**

**folk art** [fōk ärt] A style of art made by people who have had little formal training in art. (page 133)

**foreground** [fôr′ground] The part of an artwork that seems closest to the viewer. (page 148)

**form** [fôrm] An object that has height, width, and depth. (page 108)

**forms**

**found object** [found ob′jikt] A common object that has a specific purpose. Found objects are often used in assemblages. (page 189)

**G**

**geometric shape** [jē•ə•met′rik shāp] A shape, such as a triangle or a circle, that has regular outlines. (page 32)

**gesture drawing** [jes′chər drô′ing] A sketch created with loose arm movements. (page 98)

**gray scale** [grā skāl] The range of values from pure black to pure white. (page 72)

**gray scale**

**H**

**horizon line** [hə•rī′zən līn] A line that shows where the sky meets the land or the water. (page 153)

**I**

**impasto** [im•pas′tō] A technique of painting that creates a bumpy surface by using thick brushstrokes. (page 70)

**implied line** [im•plīd′ līn] A line that is suggested rather than drawn. (page 29)

**implied lines**

**Impressionism** [im•pre′shə•ni•zəm] An art movement of the late nineteenth century in which artists painted the way light and color looked at a certain moment in time. (page 68)

**L**

**landscape** [land′skāp] A painting of an outdoor scene. (page 28)

**linear perspective** [li′nē•ər pər•spek′tiv] A technique used to create a sense of depth in a two-dimensional artwork by making parallel lines meet at a vanishing point. (page 154)

linear perspective

**middle ground** [mi′dəl ground] The part of an artwork that is between the foreground and the background. (page 148)

**monochromatic color** [mo•nə•krō•ma′tik kul′ər] A group of values of one color. (page 60)

**movement** [mo͞ov′mənt] The way a viewer's eyes travel from one element to another in an artwork. (page 158)

**mural** [myo͝or′əl] A painting that is created on a wall or ceiling. A mural can be painted on an indoor or an outdoor surface. (page 168)

**negative space** [ne′gə•tiv spās] The area in a three-dimensional artwork where material has been removed. (page 103)

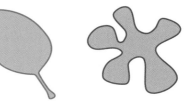

**organic shape** [ôr•gan′ik shāp] A shape that is made up of curved, irregular lines. (page 32)

organic shapes

**overlapping** [ō•vər•lap′ing] Relating to objects that are partly in front of or behind other objects. (page 48)

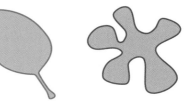

**pattern** [pa′tərn] A design made up of repeated lines, shapes, or colors. (page 118)

**plein air** [plān âr] The practice of painting outdoors; from the French for "open air." (page 69)

**Pop Art** [pop ärt] A twentieth-century art movement that was inspired by popular media, such as comic books and advertisements. (page 192)

**portrait** [pôr′trət] An artwork that shows what a person, a group of people, or an animal looks like. (page 88)

**portrait**

**positive space** [pä′zə•tiv spās] The raised part of a three-dimensional artwork. (page 103)

**primary colors** [prī′mâr•ē kul′ərz] The colors red, yellow, and blue. They are mixed together to create the other colors on the color wheel. (page 38)

**radial balance** [rā′dē•əl ba′ləns] A type of balance in which a pattern extends from the center of the artwork, like the spokes of a wheel. (page 129)

**radial balance**

**relief sculpture** [ri•lēf′ skulp′chər] A three-dimensional artwork in which part of the image stands out from the background surface. (page 102)

**rhythm** [ri′thəm] The visual beat created by repeated lines, shapes, colors, or patterns. (page 99)

**seascape** [sē′skāp] An outdoor scene that shows the sea and sky. (page 42)

**secondary colors** [se′kən•dâr•ē kul′ərz] The colors orange, green, and violet. Each one is created by combining two primary colors. (page 39)

**self-portrait** [self•pôr′trət] An artwork of a person, made by that person. (page 90)

**shade** [shād] A darker value of a color, created by mixing black and the color. (page 59)

**shades**

**silkscreen** [silk′skrēn] A printing process in which ink is forced through silk onto paper, cloth, or another surface. (page 192)

**space** [spās] The area around, between, and within objects. (page 148)

**still life** [stil līf] An artwork that shows objects arranged together in an interesting way. (page 48)

**subtractive method**
[səb•trak′tiv meth′əd] A sculpting method in which the artist cuts away, or subtracts, some of the original material. (page 102)

**Surrealism** [sə•rē′ə•li•zəm] An art style that shows impossible, dreamlike images. (page 182)

**symbol** [sim′bəl] A picture or object that stands for an idea. (page 138)

**symmetrical balance**
[sə•me′tri•kəl ba′ləns] The type of balance created when the left and right sides of an artwork match. (page 122)

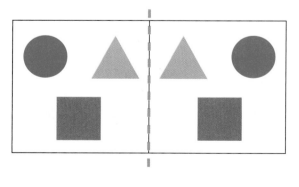

**symmetrical balance**

(T)

**tactile texture** [tak′təl teks′chər] The way the surface of a real object feels when you touch it. (page 62)

**tapestry** [tap′is•trē] A type of weaving that has colorful designs or scenes in it. (page 119)

**terra-cotta** [ter•ə•kot′ə] A type of reddish-brown clay that can be used in sculptures. (page 109)

**three-dimensional** [thrē•də•men′shə•nəl] Having height, width, and depth. (page 80)

**tint** [tint] A lighter value of a color, created by mixing white and the color. (page 59)

**tints**

**trompe l'oeil** [trômp loi] A style of painting that seems to show a three-dimensional scene on a two-dimensional surface; from the French for "trick the eye." (page 170)

**U**

**unity** [yōōʹnə•tē] A sense that an artwork is complete. (page 158)

**V**

**value** [valʹyōō] The lightness or darkness of a color. (page 59)

**vanishing point** [vanʹish•ing point] The point on the horizon line where parallel lines meet. (page 154)

**vanishing point**

**variety** [və•rīʹə•tē] A design principle used to add interest in an artwork by including different objects or art elements. (page 183)

**vertical axis** [vûrʹti•kəl akʹsəs] An invisible line that divides the left and right sides of an image. (page 122)

**vertical axis**

**visual texture** [vizhʹōō•əl teksʹchər] The appearance of texture on a drawn or painted surface. (page 62)

**visual weight** [vizhʹōō•əl wāt] The emphasis given to each side of an artwork. Artists use visual weight to create a sense of balance. (page 130)

**W**

**warm colors** [wôrm kulʹərz] The colors red, yellow, and orange. These colors create a feeling of warmth and energy. (page 43)

**weaving** [wēʹving] A cloth created from fibers that have been interlaced, or woven together. (page 118)

# Art History
## Time Line

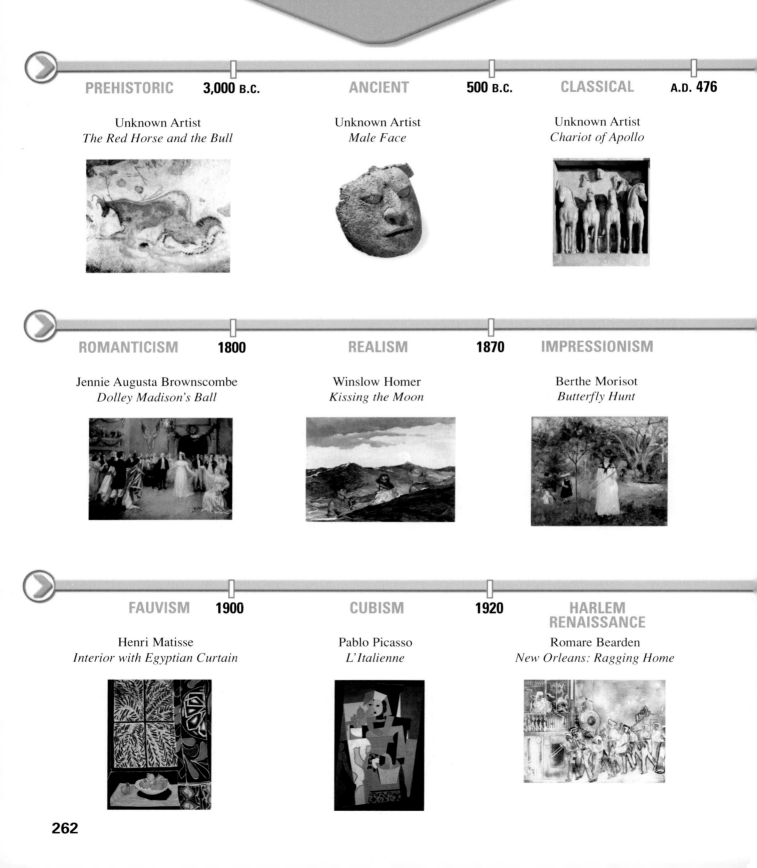

**PREHISTORIC**     **3,000** B.C.

Unknown Artist
*The Red Horse and the Bull*

**ANCIENT**     **500** B.C.

Unknown Artist
*Male Face*

**CLASSICAL**     **A.D. 476**

Unknown Artist
*Chariot of Apollo*

**ROMANTICISM**     **1800**

Jennie Augusta Brownscombe
*Dolley Madison's Ball*

**REALISM**     **1870**

Winslow Homer
*Kissing the Moon*

**IMPRESSIONISM**

Berthe Morisot
*Butterfly Hunt*

**FAUVISM**     **1900**

Henri Matisse
*Interior with Egyptian Curtain*

**CUBISM**     **1920**

Pablo Picasso
*L'Italienne*

**HARLEM RENAISSANCE**

Romare Bearden
*New Orleans: Ragging Home*

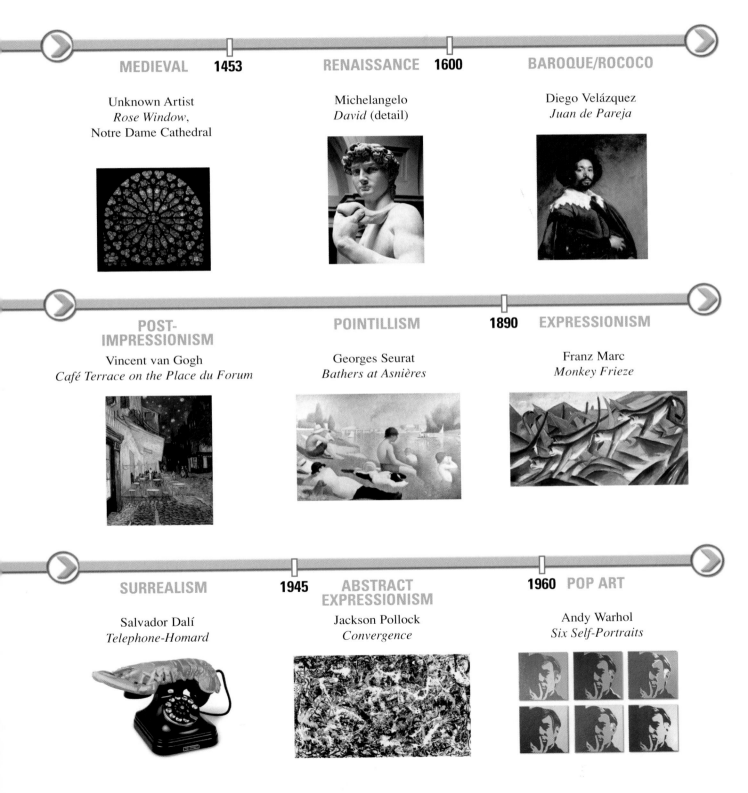

**MEDIEVAL** **1453** **RENAISSANCE** **1600** **BAROQUE/ROCOCO**

Unknown Artist
*Rose Window*,
Notre Dame Cathedral

Michelangelo
*David* (detail)

Diego Velázquez
*Juan de Pareja*

**POST-
IMPRESSIONISM** **POINTILLISM** **1890** **EXPRESSIONISM**

Vincent van Gogh
*Café Terrace on the Place du Forum*

Georges Seurat
*Bathers at Asnières*

Franz Marc
*Monkey Frieze*

**SURREALISM** **1945** **ABSTRACT
EXPRESSIONISM** **1960** **POP ART**

Salvador Dalí
*Telephone-Homard*

Jackson Pollock
*Convergence*

Andy Warhol
*Six Self-Portraits*

# Index of Artists and Artworks

# Index

# Index

cool, 42

dominant, 58

monochromatic, 60

primary, 38

secondary, 39

warm, 43

**Color scheme,** 40, 58–61

**Computer-generated art,** 198–201

**Construction,** 188–191

**Cross-Curricular Connections**

math, 154, 199

reading skills, 26–27, 52, 56–57, 82, 86–87, 112, 116–117, 142, 146–147, 172, 176–177, 202

science, 36–37, 44, 64, 66–67, 184, 196–197

social studies, 34, 40, 46–47, 50, 73, 76–77, 79, 96–97, 106–107, 119, 124, 126–127, 130, 136–137, 140, 156–157, 164, 166–167, 186–187, 193

**Cubism,** 93

## D

**Depth,** 148–151

**Distortion,** 93

**Dominant color,** 58

**Drawing,** 31, 75, 81, 91, 95, 101, 151, 155, 161, 165

## E

**Elements and Principles,** 20–23, 228–239

*See also* Elements of art; Principles of design.

**Elements of art**

color, 20, 38–41, 42–45, 58–61, 68–71, 230

form, 21, 108, 232

line, 20, 28–31, 33, 153, 228

shape, 20, 32, 34–35, 48–51, 79, 92, 229

space, 21, 103–105, 148, 233

texture, 21, 62–65, 66–67, 72–73, 231

value, 21, 59–61, 63, 69–70, 72–75, 78, 230

**Emphasis,** 78–81

**Environmental art,** 30

## F

**Facial proportion,** 89, 91

**Fiber art,** 64, 118–121

**Folk art,** 132–135

**Foreground,** 148

**Form,** 21, 108, 232

**Found objects,** 189

## G

**Geometric shape,** 32, 79

**Gesture drawing,** 98

**Glossary,** 254–261

**Gray scale,** 72

## H

**Horizon line,** 153

## I

**Impasto,** 70

**Implied line,** 29, 33

**Impressionism,** 68–71

# Index

# Acknowledgments

**Photo Credits:**

Page Placement Keys: (t)-top (c)-center (l)-left (fg)-foreground (bg)-background.

*All photos property of Harcourt except for the following:*

**Frontmatter:**

5 (tl) Roy King/Superstock; (tr) Kirstie Silverthom; 6 (tr) Artist Rights Society (ARS), New York, NY/Art Institute of Chicago, Illinois/Lauro-Giraudon, Paris/Superstock; (tc) Licensed by VAGA, New York, NY/Christopher Felver/Corbis; 7 (tl) Victoria Lantz; (tr) Caleb Cloud; 8 (tl) Charles O'Rear /Corbis; 9 (tl) Eric; 12 (tl) Francisco Matarazzo Sobrinho Collection, Sao Paulo/Superstock;  (br) Christie's Images/Superstock 14 (tr) Mark E. Gibson/Corbis; (bl) Angelo Hornak/Corbis; 15 (bl) David Woo Photo; 16 (b) The Metropolitan Museum of Art; 17 (c) Artist Rights Society (ARS), New York, NY/Cameraphoto Arte, Venice/Art Resource, NY; 18 (c) Original collage artwork by Bobbi A. Chukran, bobbichukran.com.

**Unit 1:**

25 (b) Notman Photographic Archives/McCord Museum of Canadian History, Montreal; 26 (b) (copyright) T.H. Benton and R.P. Benton Testamentray Trusts/ Licensed by VAGA, New York, NY/The Cummer Museum of Art and Gardens, Jacksonville/Superstock; 28 (b) The Grand Design, Leeds, England/Superstock; 29 (t) Artist Rights Society (ARS), New York, NY/Superstock; (b) Nardoni Galerie, Prague, Czech Republic/INDEX/Bridgeman Art Library; 30 Art (copyright) Estate of Robert Smithson/Licensed by VAGA, New York, NY/Estate of Robert Smithson, Courtesy James Cohan Gallery, New York; Collection: DIA Center for the Arts, New York; Photo by Gianfranco Gorgoni; Copyright Estate of Robert Smithson; 32 (b) Superstock; 33 (t) The J. Paul Getty Museum; 34 (tr) Artist Rights Society (ARS), New York, NY/Milwaukee Art Museum, Gift of Mrs. Harry Lynde Bradley; (bl) Kirstie Silverthom; 36 (tr, bl) Illinois State Museum; 37 (b) Caron (NPP) Philippe/Corbis Sygma; (tl) Artist Rights Society (ARS), New York, NY/The Whitney Museum of American Art; 38 (b) Paul Sierra; 39 (tr) Robert Wagstaff; 40 (c) Colleen Meechan; 42 (b) The Art Institute of Chicago; 43 (t) Tretyakov gallery, Moscow/Superstock; 44 (t) Ole Juul Hansen/Superstock; 46 (b) Artist Rights Society (ARS), New York, NY/Private Collection/Peter Willi/Superstock; (tr) Hulton/Archive; 47 (t) Artist Rights Society (ARS), New York, NY/Hamburg Kunsthalle, Hamburg, Germany/The Bridgeman Art Library; 48 (b) The Metropolitan Museum of Art, the Walter H. and Leonore Annenberg Collection, Gift of Walter H. and Leonore Annenberg, 1997, Bequest of Walter H. Annenberg, 2002. (1997.391.2) Photograph (c) 1994 the Metropolitan Museum of Art; 49 (t) Artist Rights Society (ARS), New York, NY/Cameraphoto Arte, Venice/Art Resource, NY; 50 (t) Original collage artwork by Bobbi A. Chukran, bobbichukran.com; 53 (c) Geoffrey Clements/Corbis.

**Unit 2:**

54 (t) National Gallery, London/Superstock; 55 (bl) Reunion des Musees Nationaux/Art Resource, NY; 56 (b) Artist Rights Society (ARS), New York, NY/Amon Carter Museum; 58 (b) Meredith Brooks Abbott; 59 (t) 2006 Artist Rights Society (ARS), New York/ADAGP, Paris/The Metropolitan Museum of Art, Gift of Marshall Field, 1939. (39.15) Photograph (c) 1981 The Metropolitan Museum of Art; 60 (c) Artist Rights Society (ARS), New York, NY/Norton Simon Museum, Pasadena, CA; 62 (b) The Grand Design, Leeds, England/Superstock; 63 (c) Isy Ochoa/Superstock; 64 (c) Jacksonville Museum of Modern Art, Florida/Superstock; 66 (b) Steve Vidler/Superstock; 67 (b) Harcourt Index; (tl) Mark Keller/Superstock; 68 (br, bl) Musee d'Orsay, Paris/Superstock; 69 (t) Musee d'Orsay, Paris/E.T. Archive, London/Superstock; 70 (t) Archivo Iconografico, S.A./Corbis; 72 (b) Bruce Barnbaum Photography; 73 (t) 2003 Cordon Art B.V. -Baarn-Holland; 74 (b) Matthew Alvarado; 76 (b) Artist Rights Society (ARS), New York, NY/Bridgeman Art Library, London/Superstock; 77 (br) Artist Rights Society (ARS), New York, NY/CNAC/MNAM/Dist. Reunion des Musees Nationaux/Art Resource, NY; (tl) Artist Rights Society (ARS), New York, NY/Phillips Collection, Washington, D.C./Lauros-Giraudon, Paris/Superstock; 78 (tr) Raymond Depardon/Magnum Photos; (bl) Johanna Fiore; 79 (t) Art Resource, NY/Tate Gallery, London, England; 80 (bl) (copyright) The Joseph and Robert Cornell Memorial Foundation/Licensed by VAGA, New York, NY/Art Resource; 83 (br) Artist Rights Society (ARS), New York,NY/Salvador Dali Museum, Inc.

**Unit 3:**

84 (t) Williams College Museum of Art, Museum purchase, with funds provided by the Assyrian Relief Exchange; 85 (bl) Bettmann/Corbis; 86 (bl) Feldman & Associates/ Lucy B. Campbell Gallery, London; 88 (b) David David Gallery, Philadelphia/Superstock; 89 (t) Superstock; 90(b) Christie's Images/Superstock; 92 (b) Artist Rights Society (ARS), New York, NY/Christie's Images/Superstock; 93 (tl) Artist Rights Society (ARS), New York, NY/Art Institute of Chicago, Illinois/Lauro-Giraudon, Paris/Superstock; 94 (tl) Artist Rights Society (ARS), New York, NY/Christie's Images/Superstock; (br) Anna Handelsman; 96 (tr) Bettmann/Corbis;  97 (bl) Corbis; (br) Michael Freeman/Corbis; (cr) National Portrait Gallery, Smithsonian Institution/Art Resource, NY; 98 (bl) Christie's Images/Superstock; (t) Von Der Heydt Museum, Wuppertal, Germany/Giraudon, Paris/Superstock; 99 (b) Artist Rights Society (ARS), New York, NY/National Gallery of Art, Washington D.C.; 100 (b) Artist Rights Society (ARS), New York, NY/Civica Galleria d'Arte Moderna, Milan/Fratelli Alinari/Superstock; 102 (tr) Harcourt; 103 (c) Superstock; 104 (bl) Royalty-Free/Corbis; (c) Don Couch Photography;106 (t) Christopher Felver/Corbis; (b) (copyright) Marisol/Licensed by VAGA, New York, NY/Smithsonian American Art Museum, Washington, DC/Art Resource; 107 (b) (copyright) Marisol/Licensed by VAGA, New York, NY/Albright-Knox

# Acknowledgments

Art Gallery/Corbis; 108 (t) Musee du Louvre, Paris/Superstock; 109(cr) Tomb of Qin shi Huang Di, Xianyang, China/33Bridgeman Art Library; 110 (bl) Artist Rights Society (ARS), New York, NY/Christie's Images/Superstock; (tr) Buffalo Bill Historical Center, Cody, WY, Gift of The Coe Foundation;113 (c) Artist Rights Society (ARS), New York, NY/Menil Foundation, Houston, Texas/Lauros-Giraudon, Paris/Superstock.

**Unit 4:**

114 (t) Philadelphia Museum of Art; 115 (bl) Grace Matthews/FaithRinggold.com; 116 (cl) Philadelphia Museum of Art/Corbis; (br) Christie's Images/Corbis; 118 (bl) Lowe Art Museum/Superstock; (br) The British Museum; 119 (t) Lowe Art Museum/Superstock; 120 Hailey Marosi; 122 (b) Peabody Museum, Harvard University N36551; 123 (tr) Christie's Images/Superstock; 124 (tr) The Detroit Institute of Arts; (bl) Caleb Cloud; 126 (bl) Francisco Matarazzo Sobrinho Collection, Sao Paulo/Superstock; (b) Christie's Images/Superstock; (br) Superstock; 127 (tl) Artist Rights Society (ARS), New York, NY/Christie's Images/Superstock; 128 (c) Museum of Internaitonal Folk Art/Museum of New Mexico Girard Foundation Collection, Photo: Michel Monteaux; 129 (t) Bernie Jendrzejczak; 130 (tr) Rudy Gomez Photo Arts/Collection of Carmen Lomas Garza; 132 (b) Chisholm Gallery, West Palm Beach, Florida/Superstock; 133 (t) Christie's Images/Superstock; 134 (cr) Philadelphia Museum of Art/Corbis; 136 (c) San Antonio Art League Museum; 137 (br) (copyright) Richard Haas/Licensed by VAGA, New York, NY/National Cowgirl Museum & Hall of Fame/Fort Worth, Texas; (t) Rhonda Hole/National Cowgirl Museum & Hall of Fame, Fort Worth, Texas; 138 (br) Christie's Images/Superstock; 139 (t) Warren Kimble/Kimble House; 140 (c) Burstein Collection/Corbis; 143 (br) Earlie Hudnall, Jr./Hazel Biggers.

**Unit 5:**

144 (t) Gustave Caillebotte, French, 1848-1894, Paris Street; Rainy Day, 1877, oil on canvas, 212.2 x 276.2 cm, Charles H. and Mary F.S. Worcester Collection/The Art Institute of Chicago; 145 (bl) Erich Lessing/Art Resource, NY; 146 (bl) Christie's Images/Superstock; 148 (b) Christie's Images/Corbis; 149 (l) Superstock; 150 (c) Jack Gunter; Corbis; 152 (l) The Art Archive; 153 (t) National Gallery of Scotland, Edinburgh; 154 (c) Louis K. Meisel Gallery/Corbis; 156 (b) Ben Mangor/Superstock; 157 (tl) George H. H. Huey/Corbis; (cr) San Antonio Missions National Historical Park; 158 (b) Superstock; 159 (t) Roy King/Superstock; 160 (t) Lisa Quinones/Black Star; 162 (bl) Nathan Benn/Corbis; 163 (t) Steve Vidler/Superstock; 164 (t) Superstock; 166 (b) Bill Ross/Corbis; (cl) Phil Huber/Stock Photo; 167 (c) Art on File/Corbis; 168 (b) Charles O'Rear Corbis; 169 (t) Meg Saligman; 170 (c) RJD Enterprises; 173 (br) Burstein Collection/Corbis.

**Unit 6:**

174 (t) Artist Rights Society (ARS), New York, NY/AFP/Corbis; (bg) Royalty-Free/Corbis; 175 AP/Wide World Photos; 176 (br) Kactus Foto, Santiago, Chile/Superstock; 178 (b) Artist Rights Society (ARS), New York, NY/Albright-Knox Art Gallery/Corbis; 179 (t) Geoffrey Clements/Corbis; 180 (tr) Artist Rights Society (ARS), New York, NY/Burstein Collection/Corbis; (bl) Eric; 182 (b) Artist Rights Society (ARS), New York,

NY/Christie's Images/Superstock; 183 (tr) Artist Rights Society (ARS), New York, NY/Superstock; 184 (t) Artist Rights Society (ARS), New York,NY/Christie's Images/Superstock; 186 (bl) Courtesy of the Southeastern Center for Contemporary Art (SECCA), Winston-Salem, NC, Photo by Jackson Smith/Maya Lin Studio; (tl) Layne Kennedy/Corbis; 187 (b) Balthazar Korab/Maya Lin Studio; (cr) James P. Blair/Corbis; 188 (b) Artist Rights Society (ARS), New York, NY/Solomon R. Guggenheim Museum, New York, gift, Mr. & Mrs. Sidney Singer, 1977, photo by Robert E. Mates; 189 (tl) Albright-Knox Art Gallery/Corbis; 190 (t) (copyright) The Joseph and Robert Cornell Memorial Foundation/Licensed by VAGA, New York, NY/Geoffrey Clements/Corbis; 192 (b) Artist Rights Society (ARS), New York, NY/Burstein Collection/Corbis; 193 (t) Geoffrey Clements/Corbis; 194 (c) (copyright) Wayne Thiebaud/Licensed by VAGA, New York, NY/Christie's Images/Corbis; 196 (tl) Eranian PH/Corbis Sygma; (br) Lowell Georgia/Corbis;197 (br) General Motors Corporation; (t) Durand Patrick/Corbis Sygma; 198 (b) Angelo Di Cicco/Museum of Computer Art; 199 (tr) Joan Myerson Shrager/Museum of Computer Art; 200 (t) Museum of Computer Art; 203 (cl) Artist Rights Society (ARS), New York, NY/National Museum of Modern Art, Paris, France/Lauros-Giraudon, Paris/Superstock.

**Backmatter:**

**Gallery of Artists:**

240 (tl) Duncan H. Abbott/Meredith Abbott; (cl) Norton Simon Museum, Pasadena, CA; (bl) Artists Rights Society (ARS), NY/Roger-Viollet, Paris/Bridgeman Art Library; (tr) Bruce Barnbaum; (cr) Bettmann/Corbis; (br) PictureHistory; 241 (tl) Earlie Hudnall Jr.; (cl) Corbis; (tr) H.O. Havemeyer Collection, Bequest of Mrs. H.O. Havemeyer, 1929/Metropolitan Museum of Art; (cr) Erich Lessing/Art Resource, NY; (cr) Original collage artwork by Bobbi A. Chukran, bobbichukran.com; (br) Angelo Di Cicco; 242 (tl) John Clive; (cl) Smithsonian American Art Museum, Washington, DC/Art Resource, NY; (cl) Gianni Dagli Ort/Corbis; (bl) AP/Wide World Photos; (tr) Giraudon/Art Resource, NY; (cr) Robert S. Duncanson, artist, Montreal, QC, 1864. I-11978; Notman Photographic Archives, McCord Museum of Canadian History, Montreal; (cr) Raymond Depardon/Magnum Photos; 243 (cl) M.C. Escher's "Selfportrait" © 2003 Cordon Art B.V. - Baarn - Holland. All rights reserved; (bl) Christopher Felver/Corbis; (tr) Sarah Campbell Blaffer Foundation, Houston, TX/Artists Rights Society (ARS), NY/AKG Images; (cr) Boterell Roy/Corbis Sygma; (br) Christopher Felver/Corbis; 244 (cl) AKG Images; (bl) The Barnes Foundation, Merion Station, Pennsylvania/Corbis; (tr) The Barnes Foundation, Merion Station, Pennsylvania/Corbis; (cr) Images of Yale individuals (RU684). Papers, Manuscripts and Archives, Yale University Library; (cr) Getty Images; (br) Karla Matzke/Jack Gunter; 245 (tl) Superstock; (cl) Corbis; (bl) Peter Harholdt/Corbis; (tr) Rufus F. Folkks/Corbis; (cr) Bettmann/Corbis; (br) Nina Hauser Swanson/Don Jacot; 246 (tl) Artists Rights Society (ARS), NY/AKG Images; (cl) Bettmann/Corbis; (bl) National Museum of Modern Art, Paris, France/Lauros-Giraudon, Paris/Superstock; (tr) Edward Loedding/Kimble House, Inc.; (cr) Edward Loedding/Kimble House, Inc.; (br) Hulton Archive/Getty Images; 247 (tl) Christopher Felver/Corbis; (bl) Layne

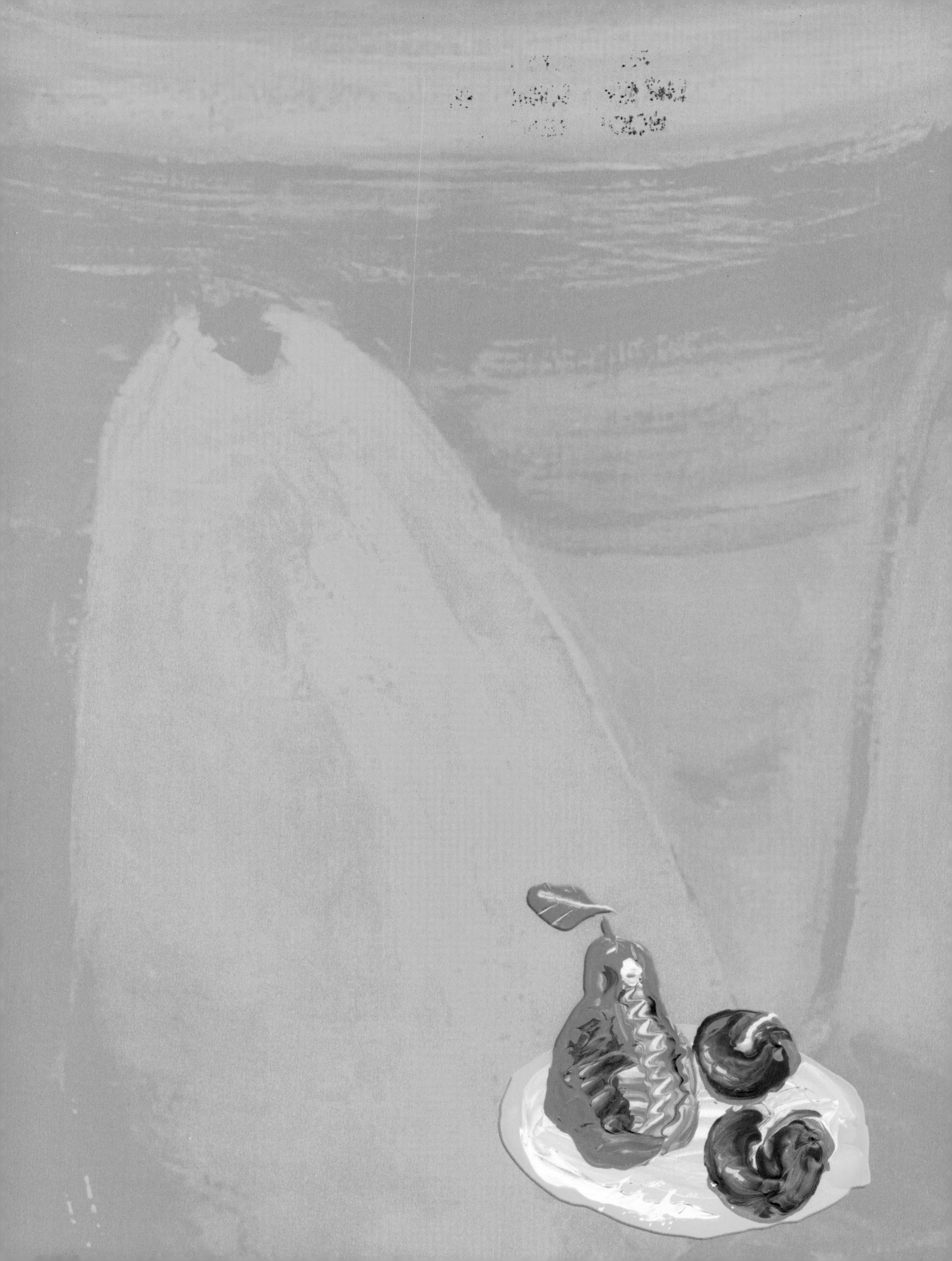